ENHANCING YOUR CHILD'S BEHAVIOR

A Step-by-Step Guide for Parents and Teachers

Robert Evert Cimera

A SCARECROWEDUCATION BOOK

The Scarecrow Press, Inc.
Lanham, Maryland, and Oxford
2003

A SCARECROWEDUCATION BOOK

Published in the United States of America
by Scarecrow Press, Inc.
A Member of the Rowman & Littlefield Publishing Group
4501 Forbes Boulevard, Suite 200, Lanham, MD 20706
www.scarecroweducation.com

PO Box 317
Oxford
OX2 9RU, UK

British Library Cataloguing in Publication Information Available

Library of Congress Cataloging-in-Publication Data

Cimera, Robert E.
   Enhancing your child's behavior : a step-by-step guide for parents and
teachers / Robert Evert Cimera.
       p. cm.
   "A SCARECROWEDUCATION BOOK."
   ISBN 0-8108-4757-4 (pbk. : alk. paper)
   1. Behavior modification—Handbooks, manuals, etc. 2. Educational
psychology—Handbooks, manuals, etc. 3. Classroom
management—Handbooks, manuals, etc. 4. Children—Conduct of
life—Handbooks, manuals, etc. I. Title.
LB1060.2.C55 2003
371.39'3—dc21   2003001287

♾™ The paper used in this publication meets the minimum requirements of
American National Standard for Information Sciences—Permanence of
Paper for Printed Library Materials, ANSI/NISO Z39.48-1992.
Manufactured in the United States of America.

CONTENTS

PREFACE

People are judged not only by what they know but also by how they act. Because of this, being able to teach children how to behave appropriately is the cornerstone of effective educational programs as well as their future success. After all, just imagine how far people would get in the adult world if they refused to show up for work on time, never did what they were told, got up and walked around during important meetings, or did not get along with other people.

Whether you are a teacher of several dozen children, or a parent of one, this book will walk you through a simple, step-by-step process that will help you:

- determine why your children act the way they do,
- develop strategies to reward appropriate behavior,
- develop strategies to discourage inappropriate behavior,
- implement effective behavior modification programs, and
- learn methods for assessing whether your strategies are working.

This book also has chapters on how to help children with specific behavior problems, such as

- Hyperactivity
- Inattentiveness
- Stereotypic behavior
- Withdrawn behavior
- Temper tantrums, and
- Violent behavior

THE BASICS OF BEHAVIOR CHANGE

CHAPTER OBJECTIVES

By the time you complete this chapter, you should be able to:

- Define behavior.
- Explain why defining behavior is important.
- List some of the primary causes of behavior.
- Discuss how defining "appropriate" behavior can be problematic.
- Define behavioral modification.
- Explain ethical considerations involved when changing somebody's behavior.
- Define key terms.

CASE STUDY OF ROBBIE WARNER

Mr. and Mrs. Warner sat around a small table, talking to their child's teacher during their parent-teacher conference.

"I don't know what to do with him," Mrs. Warner said after Miss Radagast confirmed her worst fears. "Robbie is a bright child. He is a good child."

"I am not saying that he isn't a wonderful little boy," Miss Radagast insisted, not for the first or last time. "I am just saying that his behavior is getting a little out of hand. He doesn't sit still, he frequently gets out of his seat, he talks back to me when I tell him to behave, and he is somewhat of a bully on the playground."

Mr. Warner nodded and his wife looked at the ground. "We have noticed those same behaviors at home. We frankly do not know what to do. I know he can behave better. It is just that he chooses to act up. We were hoping that you would give us some ideas on how to handle him."

"I would suggest developing some sort of behavioral modification program," Miss Radagast replied, trying to sound as reassuring as possible.

"A behavioral modification program!" Mrs. Warner gasped. "Isn't that a bit severe? I mean, he is a bit active and naughty, but I don't want him to be shocked or drugged or anything."

Miss Radagast smiled. "No, that isn't what I mean. I am talking about looking at his behaviors and developing ways of making Robbie do what we want him to do."

"I'm not too sure that is what I want," Mr. Warner said politely. "I mean, yes, I do want him to treat people better and to stop disrupting your class, but I was hoping that we would teach him right from wrong, not simply to do what he was told like an automaton."

"Right," Mrs. Warner added. "He should be able to think about what he is doing and do what is right, not just because he is afraid of being spanked or suspended."

"Well, we can certainly come to some sort of agreement as to what behaviors we should focus on."

"Then what is our first step?" Mrs. Warner asked. "What do we do?"

Miss Radagast reached over to her bookshelf and pulled out a small book. Handing it to the Warners, she said, "Start by reading this. It talks about how to modify behavior in a very simple, step-by-step process."

CASE STUDY QUESTIONS

After reading the case study and this chapter, you should be able to answer the following questions. We will return to the case study and discuss these questions at the end of the chapter.

Question 1: According to Mr. Warner, what appears to be causing Robbie's behavior?

Question 2: How does Mrs. Warner appear to define behavioral modification?

Question 3: What are some of the ethical considerations that the Warners seem to have regarding using behavioral modification?

INTRODUCTION

If you are reading this book, you probably are either a parent or a teacher. Moreover, you probably are also very concerned about the behavior of one of your children or students. Perhaps the child runs around uncontrollably, doesn't listen to what you say, does things that are unsafe, or is violent with other people. Maybe he or she is just driving you crazy! Most likely, you have tried various punishments. Perhaps you have tried some sort of reward system. You might have even begged and pleaded with your child to behave appropriately. Did these strategies work?

The purpose of this book is to outline, in very easy-to-understand terms, the principles behind, and steps to, changing behavior. Throughout this book, we discuss how to:

- identify problem behaviors,
- determine what is causing the problem behaviors, and
- replace problem behaviors with those that are more appropriate.

We also present strategies for changing behaviors, including those that are violent, withdrawn, or hyperactive.

DEFINING "BEHAVIOR"

Before we can talk about how to change your child's behavior, we must first define what behavior is. So what do you think "behavior" is? Can you define it? It is probably more difficult than you thought.

Behavior As a Measurable Phenomenon

There are numerous definitions of behavior in the fields of psychology and education. Most indicate that behavior is an observable phenomenon, such as hitting somebody over the head with a baseball bat or typing on a computer. With such definitions, emotions are not considered behaviors. "Feeling sad" is not a behavior, since the actual feeling is not observable. You might be able to see behaviors caused by the sadness, such as crying, but you can't actually see the emotion.

Behavior and Inaction

Some definitions use the "dead person's principle" to define behaviors. That is, if a dead person can do it, then it isn't a behavior. Including this concept in the definition would mean that sitting still could not be a behavior since a dead person could do it. So, inaction, according to some people, cannot be considered a behavior even though it is observable.

Behavior As a Response to Stimuli

Finally, there are some people who view behavior as a response to a given stimulus, much as a plant might tilt toward the sun. In this definition, there must be something that caused the behavior, some sort of impetus or trigger. For example, a child throwing a temper tantrum is a direct response to being told that he has to go to bed. In other words, there is always a cause or an antecedent to the behavior.

A Working Definition of Behavior

For our purposes, we consider behavior to be an observable action. But we also include things that a dead person can do, such as being quiet or staring off into space. We also consider behaviors that do not have an overt trigger, such as vocal tics. Moreover, we also take into consideration the underlying emotions that can cause your child to behave the way he or she does.

THE IMPORTANCE OF DEFINING BEHAVIOR

You are probably thinking, "Who cares how behavior is defined? Let's get to the good stuff. Help me figure out what to do with my kid!" Don't worry. The good stuff is right around the corner.

We have to define behavior for a number of reasons. First, it is important to understand the complexity of what we are talking about. Whereas you might want to stop your child from picking on her little sister, other people might want to stop their children from setting fires or killing animals. Other parents might be trying to encourage their children to be more social. By their very nature, behaviors are extremely diverse. So thinking about the definition of behavior will broaden how you view your child.

Second, without defining behavior, you might have a tendency to focus on the wrong thing. For example, you might have picked up this book because you are getting very frustrated by your child. However, that isn't your child's behavior. It is actually *your* emotion.

Throughout this book, we follow a step-by-step process that will help you help your child. You will be asked to think about your child and then write down specific things that you want to change. To help your child, you will have to understand the difference between your child's behavior and your reaction to the behavior.

CAUSES OF BEHAVIOR

At this point, you may be thinking to yourself, "Why do my children do the things that they do?" This is an excellent question! After all, it would be difficult to modify your children's behaviors if you do not first understand why the behaviors are occurring. However, as we discuss at length in chapter 4, determining the cause of behavior is easier said than done. For instance, many times people do not know why they do things. This is particularly true if your child is very young or has a disability, such as mental retardation or attention deficit hyperactivity disorder (ADHD).

Think about it for a moment. Do you know why you do *everything* that you do? Why do you look at a car wreck as you drive pass? Why do you peek through your fingers when you know that something scary is about to happen in the movie that you are watching? Why do you fidget in your chair when somebody is talking about something boring or painful? The causes of your behaviors, and the behaviors of your children, are not always easily explainable. Moreover, the explanations that we might actually give for our behavior may not always be the correct ones.

Even though it is difficult to understand the cause of people's behaviors, we must first understand what we are trying to change. Consider this example. Suppose that you have a child who gets up and wanders around during dinner or class. You tell him to sit down, which he does, but seconds later he jumps up and wanders around the table again.

If you believe that your child is not doing what he should do out of spite or to get you angry, you will probably address his behavior much differently than if you believe that he is actually trying to be good but can't due to physiological reasons. Perhaps he has ADHD or temporal lobe seizures. In other words, understanding your perception of your child's behavior is the first key to changing your child's behavior. We discuss this at length in later chapters.

There are many diverse and conflicting explanations for the cause of behaviors. As the list below indicates, only a few are discussed here. For a more detailed explanation of the various philosophies regarding behavior, consult a textbook on human behavior or psychology.

- Behavior As a Natural Response to Stimuli
- Behavior As a Willful Choice
- Behavior As an Interaction with the Environment
- Behavior As an Outcome of Biology
- Behavior As a Multifaceted Outcome

Behavior As a Natural Response to Stimuli

As mentioned previously, many people speak of behavior as a natural response to a given stimulus. For example, if you banged your head you would probably cry out in pain. You most likely didn't think about your response to the situation; you just reacted naturally. The same is true if you saw something startling from the corner of your eye. You probably would look at it without any real thought about your actions.

Behavior As a Willful Choice

Others people talk about behavior as a willful process in which individuals choose to act the way they do. For example, if you bang your head, some people would insist that you chose to respond the way you did. You could have remained quiet or grumbled to yourself. You could have yelled. Further, what you yelled was completely up to you. You could have said "Ow!" or "Darn it!" or you could have used profanity. The same is true for being distracted by something that entered the edge of your vision. Some people would say that you didn't have to look, but you chose to.

Traditionally, people who believe that behavior is the result of a willful choice see behavior as a way for people to get something, avoid something, or both. For instance, a student who causes a disruption in class might be trying to get attention or recognition from his peers. He might also be trying to avoid the schoolwork that the teacher might assign. Figuring out what exactly your child is trying to get or avoid will be a key step in trying to change his or her behavior.

Behavior As an Interaction with the Environment

Still others consider that behavior is a function of the interaction between the person and his or her environment or upbringing. For example, if you grew up in a home where it was okay to swear, you would probably be more likely to curse when you banged your head. Or if you were taught to be aware of your surroundings for safety reasons, then this may be why you look at things such as car accidents.

Behavior As an Outcome of Biology

Some people feel that behavior is heavily determined by biological forces, such as those involving heredity. For example, many people think that boys are naturally energetic or more independent than are girls, or that girls are more social than are boys. Moreover, behavior is often influenced by biological factors. For instance, suicide might be triggered by depression, which could be caused by a chemical imbalance in the brain. In other words, from this perspective, behavior is often heavily influenced by factors that are within our biological makeup and not necessarily by environment or by the person's choice.

Behavior As a Multifaceted Outcome

Perhaps the most accepted explanation for the cause of behaviors is that all of the above form a complex web of interactions. For example, genetics might make somebody tend to be short tempered. Further, the person's environment might be stressful, thus increasing the likelihood of a certain response. Moreover, due to his or her upbringing, the person might believe that it is appropriate to use profanity.

Defining Appropriate Behavior

Perhaps the most important question you have is, "What is 'appropriate' behavior?" or "How should my child behave?" For example, when is teasing age-appropriate, and when is it being mean or immature? How about defying authority figures? When is talking back to parents problematic, and when is it simply part of the gaining of independence typically associated with adolescence?

Certainly what is considered "appropriate" behavior is extremely subjective and difficult to define. Not only is appropriateness determined largely by personal perspective, but it is heavily influenced by cultural and generational expectations as well as the particular situation. Moreover, no one behavior is always appropriate or inappropriate. Consider a ten year old who is screaming at the top of her lungs. Is this appropriate behavior? Well, it depends. What if she is in severe pain? Or if a stranger is trying to force her into his car? What if she is simply upset and throwing a temper tantrum? Or if she is just excited?

Clearly what is deemed appropriate depends on a multitude of factors. However, without a clear understanding of how it is you want your child to behave, it will be very difficult for you to help him or her achieve your goal. This is particularly true for students with mental retardation who might not realize the subtle nuances of how to behave. For example, suppose that you have a child with mental retardation and you teach her that she should never let anybody touch her "private parts." It is very likely that she will overgeneralize what you have taught her so that she will not allow doctors to perform basic physical examinations. What about a child who is taught not to talk to strangers? Would he be able to discern when talking to strangers, such as police officers, is appropriate? How about when is it appropriate to tell the truth and when "white lies" are acceptable?

Are you starting to see how difficult defining appropriate behavior is? If you cannot define the exact behavior that you want your children to perform, how can you expect them to know what is expected of them? To help teach your child how to behave, you must carefully think about the behaviors that you want to teach him or her as well as the situations in which those behaviors may or may not be appropriate. We discuss this issue at length in chapter 3.

DEFINING BEHAVIORAL MODIFICATION

This is a good point at which to define "behavioral modification." *Behavioral modification* describes a systematic approach to looking at behavior. It involves identifying why the behavior is occurring or not occurring. It looks at what factors influence behaviors and how these factors can be manipulated so that the behavior occurs or doesn't occur at the desired times and places.

Behavioral modification is a very applied research process. Throughout this book, you will be asked to think about various things and brainstorm answers to many questions. It is immensely important that you complete these exercises. If you don't, you will limit your chances of successfully changing your child's behavior.

THE ETHICS OF BEHAVIORAL MODIFICATION

What comes to mind when you hear the term "behavioral modification?" You might think of shock therapy or mood-altering drugs or brainwashing. Consequently, the topic might make you a bit apprehensive. After all, in the final analysis, behavioral modification is manipulating somebody to do something that you want him or her to do. Is this bad? Not in and of itself. After all, children do not know how to behave naturally. Instinct does not tell them to be quiet in the library or to sit in their chairs while taking a test or to cross the street when the sign says "walk." So it is up to teachers and parents to educate children on how to behave. Still, this responsibility should not be taken lightly. There is considerable opportunity for abuse.

How do you know if you might be abusing the strategies that we are going to be discussing? Please ask yourself the following questions whenever you are attempting to modify your child's behavior:

- For whose benefit are you changing the behavior?
- Does the child's behavior really need to be changed?
- Is the new behavior actually going to help the child?
- Is the new behavior simply a temporary fix to a long-term problem?
- Is the new behavior going to cause any problems?

Certainly there will be times that you need to modify your child's behavior simply to maintain your sanity. For instance, maybe your child likes to bang on pots and pans and make head-splitting noise. Clearly, this is not the type of behavior that you could endure for very long. Changing your child's behavior obviously would help you obtain some peace of mind. However, as a parent or teacher, your goal should be to help your child succeed in life, not just make your day easier—although you will need to do that as well. A person who makes noise and does not consider other people's feelings probably will not go very far in life. Rather than focusing exclusively on your needs, try to keep in mind the ultimate goal of behavioral modification: teaching children the skills they will need to succeed.

Further, you must take great care to not give children behaviors that are going to be more problematic than the ones they originally had. For instance, imagine that you taught your child to speak only when spoken to. As a result she developed "selective mutism," a condition in which children rarely speak aloud. Do you think that you actually helped your child? Probably not.

KEY BEHAVIORAL TERMS

Before we start getting into the actual process of changing behavior, there are some terms with which you should familiarize yourself:

- Target behavior
- Replacement behavior
- Frequency
- Intensity
- Duration
- Latency
- Baseline
- Intervention
- Reversal
- Antecedent
- Consequence

Target Behavior

Throughout this book we discuss your child's "target behavior." Simply put, the target behavior is the one that you want to change. A target behavior could be something that you want to decrease, such as talking back to adults. Or it can be something that you want to increase, such as the amount of time your child studies. As discussed in chapters 2 and 3, you will need to define the target behavior in very measurable terms before you begin trying to help your child.

Replacement Behavior

Sometimes you might want to completely eliminate a particular behavior (i.e., the target behavior), such as one that is violent or unsafe. However, as discussed at length in chapter 3, it is difficult to extinguish a behavior without replacing it. After all, people usually act the way they do for a reason, perhaps to satisfy a particular need, such as for attention. If you just focus on preventing the target behavior, it is likely that children will develop another, equally annoying, behavior that gets them what they want. Replacement behaviors, therefore, are what you want your child to do instead of behavior that you are trying to eliminate.

Frequency

Frequency is how often a behavior occurs. Measuring frequency is particularly important when you want to increase or decrease the number of times something happens. It is important to be able to express the frequency of behavior in the same terms so that you can compare whether the behavior is changing over time. For example, if your child gets out of her seat seven times in a 10-minute period, you could say that behavior's frequency is 42 times an hour.

Intensity

Intensity indicates the severity of a behavior. For example, let's suppose that, on occasion, your child gets very angry. He doesn't get angry a lot, so you are not concerned about frequency. After all, it is perfectly natural for kids to get upset from time to time. You are, however, very worried about how upset your child gets. Rather than just verbalizing his displeasure in an appropriate manner, he screams, hits, kicks, and throws things. In other words, it is not the frequency of the behavior that concerns you but the intensity of his behavior when it occurs.

To address the intensity of behavior, you will have to be able to distinguish the various levels of severity that the behavior comes in. So you will have to be able to distinguish a "level 2" temper tantrum from a "level 1" temper tantrum. For this reason, intensity is not an appropriate way to measure many behaviors. After all, how would you measure the intensity of somebody getting out of a chair?

Duration

Duration measures how long the behavior lasts. Again, there might be circumstances in which you do not care how often the behavior occurs or how severe the behavior is. In these cases, you might examine the behavior's duration. For instance, suppose that you are concerned about your child's studying. You could measure the number of times that she studies, but that really wouldn't help you. After all, she could be studying a hundred times a day, but her "study sessions" could only last for 10 seconds! You might consider looking at the intensity of your child's studying, but how would you measure that? In this situation, trying to increase how long your child studies might be the best approach, so you would measure the behavior's duration.

To measure duration, the behavior must have a clear beginning and ending. Perhaps you could measure the time that your child sits down at the kitchen table with her schoolwork to the time she gets up and leaves. However, keep in mind that this does not mean that she actually studied or studied well!

Latency

Let's suppose that your child does what you ask every time. The frequency of complying with your request would be 100 percent. Let's also suppose that your child does what you ask with a smile on her face and completes the task well, so you are not concerned with the intensity or duration of her behavior. However, it takes your child a long time to get started. Maybe it takes her an average of an hour before she gets around to doing her chores after you tell her to do it. In these types of situations, you would want to focus on the latency of the behavior. That is, the time it takes for the behavior to start. As with duration, to examine latency, the behavior must have a clear beginning point.

Baseline

To determine whether you are actually changing your child's target behavior, you must be able to compare your child's behavior from what it was to what it is after you try to change it. Baseline is a fancy way of indicating how your child was originally behaving. It is often displayed in the form of a graph. Determining a child's baseline is discussed in detail in chapter 4.

Intervention

Once you have figured out the frequency, intensity, duration, or latency of your child's target behavior (i.e., the baseline), you can begin to attempt to modify his or her behavior. This is done by creating some sort of intervention, or "behavioral modification program." For example, if you want to decrease the number of times your child throws a temper tantrum, you might implement a system whereby he gets a reward every day he behaves appropriately and gets punished whenever he throws things or yells. This system of reward and punishment would be your intervention. You would then determine whether the intervention is working by comparing your child's behavior after the intervention to his behavior prior to the intervention (i.e., the baseline).

Reversal

Let's suppose that you develop an intervention program that you don't want to last forever. For example, perhaps you pay your child $10 for every time she reads a book. You are trying to increase her love for reading, but you don't want it to always be contingent on getting paid. You want her to enjoy reading for its own sake, not just for the money that she receives for finishing a book. So the reward (the $10) is a way of getting her "hooked" on reading. Eventually you will take away the reward and hope that the desired behavior will continue. This is called a "reversal." You can think of it as reversing the conditions to the way they were before you intervened to see whether the behavior has stuck.

Antecedent

An antecedent is something that happened before a particular event that somehow contributed to the event. It might not have caused what happened, but it had some sort of bearing on it. For example, suppose you were asked, "What was an antecedent to you buying this book?" What would you say?

If you said that an antecedent was opening a door to the bookstore, you are missing the point a little bit. Although opening the door to the bookstore certainly occurred before you bought this book, it didn't really have much bearing on the outcome. Yes, you could argue that if you never opened the door, you could not have gotten into the store to make your purchase, but that is being nitpicky.

A better antecedent to buying this book could be that your child got in trouble at school or threw a huge temper tantrum—something that motivated you to say to yourself, "I have to change my child's behavior." That event had far more influence on you buying this book than did opening the door to the bookstore.

When we start looking at the cause of your child's behavior, determining antecedents will become very important. If you can determine the antecedents to inappropriate behaviors, you can remove them and prevent the undesirable behavior before it occurs.

Consequence

You probably already understand what a consequence is. It is what happens as a result of a given action. Each action is likely to have multiple consequences. For instance, if your child hit another child on the playground, several consequences would be likely to ensue. Your child might get suspended. The other child might get hurt. Your child might get a reputation as a mean kid. Teachers might begin to suspect that your child has a behavior disorder and should be in special education. In other words, consequences are often what motivate us to change people's behavior.

APPLYING WHAT YOU HAVE READ

Hopefully this chapter has answered some of your questions about behavioral modification. Now let's apply what you have learned. Go back to the beginning of the chapter and re-read the case study about Robbie Warner. Then try to answer the questions that appear immediately after the case study.

Question 1: According to Mr. Warner, What Appears to Be Causing Robbie's Behavior?

The first case study question involves the cause of Robbie's inappropriate behaviors. As we discussed in the chapter, behavior can be caused by many things. Understanding the cause of the behavior is going to be instrumental if the Warners are going to succeed in changing their child's behavior. Based on what you have read, what do you think Mr. Warner believes is causing Robbie to do all of these inappropriate things?

From what Mr. Warner has said, it appears that he thinks Robbie is acting inappropriately on purpose. That is to say, from his father's perspective, Robbie has a choice of whether or not to be out of his seat, arguing with his teachers, and bullying other students. It may be that Mr. Warner is wrong about this. It may be that Robbie has a disability that makes him act impulsively. Knowing the cause of the behavior is the first step in being able to improve how your child acts.

Question 2: How Does Mrs. Warner Appear to Define Behavioral Modification?

Many people hear "behavioral modification" and think about *One Flew Over the Cuckoo's Nest*. They think of mood-altering drugs or lobotomies. Consequently, many parents and teachers are reluctant to use behavioral modification strategies to help improve the behavior of their children. Look back at Mrs. Warner's reaction when behavioral modification is first brought up. How do you think she defines behavioral modification?

Clearly, Mrs. Warner doesn't have a favorable view of behavioral modification. Apparently, the first thing that entered her mind was shock therapy. Yes, shock therapy and other aversive procedures have been used to change how people act; however, there are many less harmful ways to achieve that goal. Before the Warners begin to develop a behavioral modification plan to help their son, they are going to have to broaden their view of what behavioral modification is.

Question 3: What Are Some of the Ethical Considerations That the Warners Seem to Have Regarding Using Behavioral Modification?

Perhaps the most important topic covered in this chapter is the ethical considerations that must be addressed before a behavioral modification program is developed. Changing people's behavior can have lifelong repercussions and should be taken very seriously. Further, some of these repercussions can be extremely detrimental to the person whose behavior is being changed. So what are some of the ethical considerations that the Warners will have to consider before they develop a behavioral modification program for their son?

Clearly, there are many ethical implications for changing Robbie's behavior. However, one that was voiced in the case study was the outcome of the program. Specifically, Robbie's parents were not entirely happy with the thought of making their son totally compliant with everybody's demands. Instead, the Warners want Robbie to be able to tell right from wrong and then make the appropriate decision. This is very important since making children follow the orders of adults without thinking could produce individuals who are easily taken advantage of.

THE PROCESS OF MODIFYING BEHAVIOR

CHAPTER OBJECTIVE

By the time you complete this chapter, you should be able to:

- List the steps taken to modify your child's behavior.

CASE STUDY OF KATIE PEARSON

CRASH! Another cup is destined for the garbage pile. This was the third thing that Katie Pearson had broken this week. Broken pieces of glass were everywhere. Katie looked at her mother. Her mother looked at Katie. Almost immediately the argument began.

"Get to your room this very instant!" Mrs. Pearson yelled. "I have had as much of this as I can take, young lady!"

"But mom!" Katie protested, "I didn't do it on purpose!"

"That is what you always say," Mrs. Pearson replied bitterly as she got out the well-used dustpan. "That is what you said for the other two cups that you 'accidentally' dropped on the floor. As a matter of fact, that is what you said when you broke the fish tank that you were supposed to be cleaning it out. I think that you are just trying to get me angry."

"But it was heavy! And wet! It slipped out of my hands!"

"I suppose that the picture frame was also too heavy. And the vase that you broke last month! If I told you once, I told you a hundred times, don't touch that vase. But no, you had to pick it up and now your grand-mother's vase is broken too."

"I am sorry. I said that I was sorry about that. I didn't mean to break it."

"You know," Mrs. Pearson said as she bent down to sweep up the shards of broken glass, "we are going to have to do something about this. I am tired of cleaning up after you. You are going to destroy this entire house and everything in it."

"I'm sorry," Katie said weakly.

"I know. Every time you break something you have to pay me to re-place it. The vase alone was worth over three hundred dollars."

"I can't afford that!"

"You can if you get a job. Maybe a paper route or mowing lawns. Al-though heaven knows that you would break the lawn mower, too."

"I don't do it on purpose. I am just accident prone."

"Further, you will not be getting any allowance until you pay for the cups, picture frame, and the vase."

"But what if I never am able to pay you back?"

CASE STUDY QUESTIONS

After reading the case study and this chapter, you should be able to an-swer the following questions. We will return to the case study and dis-cuss these questions at the end of the chapter.

Question 1: What is the target behavior that Mrs. Pearson is focusing on?

Question 2: According to Mrs. Pearson, why is Katie performing the target behavior?

Question 3: Other than willful choice on her part, what other causes could explain Katie's behavior?

INTRODUCTION

You are probably wondering, "How do I make my child's behavior more appropriately?" Regardless of the behavior in question, the process is relatively the same. In this chapter we discuss the steps that you will need to take to modify behavior. These steps include the following (see figure 2.1):

- Step 1: Identifying the target and replacement behaviors
- Step 2: Collecting baseline data and determining the cause of the target behavior
- Step 3: Developing an intervention to increase appropriate behavior
- Step 4: Developing an intervention to decrease inappropriate behavior
- Step 5: Implementing and evaluating the intervention
- Step 6: Implementing new strategies if needed

STEP 1: IDENTIFYING THE TARGET AND REPLACEMENT BEHAVIORS

As we discussed in chapter 1, the target behavior is what you want to change. For instance, suppose that your child sits around all day and watches television. Or maybe he argues with you when you tell him to do something. These are the behaviors that you want to reduce. Having your child playing with peers or saying "thank you" might be target behaviors that you want to increase.

Also in this step, you will need to determine what behavior you want your child to perform. That is, what behavior will replace the behavior you are trying to change? Like determining the cause of the target behavior, identifying the replacement behavior is essential. For example, let's suppose that you want to stop your child from biting. So you go through the process that we are discussing and get him to stop biting. But now he is hitting. You see, modifying behavior is not just about stopping inappropriate actions, but also teaching the correct behavior. Please keep this in mind! You are not just saying "No! Don't do that!" You are taking the time to teach your child how to behave the way that he or she should.

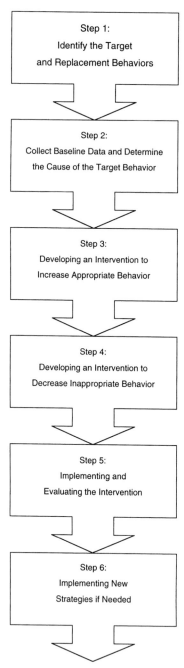

Figure 2.1 The Behavioral Change Process

Identifying the replacement behavior is not as difficult as identifying the cause of the target behavior, but it is still tricky. This is especially true when children have mental retardation and do not completely understand when and where they should be performing the replacement behavior.

For example, suppose that you have a daughter who frequently gets into fights with boys. You think that she is doing this to feel in charge. So you develop a program that decreases her fighting behavior and increases a more appropriate way of being in charge, such as coordinating games played during recess. Perhaps you yell and punish her whenever she fights with boys and reward her whenever she plays nicely.

The question that you should think about is, "Is there ever a time when the behavior that I am replacing is okay?" In other words, is fighting ever an appropriate behavior? Before you say, "No. There are always alternatives to fighting. I never want my child to fight," imagine that your daughter was being raped or abducted. Should she fight back?

The trick to replacing behavior is not to completely repress it but to teach children when and where it is appropriate to display these behaviors. So rather than say, "Never do this!" or "Never do that!"—think very carefully about what you actually want your child to do. Do you really mean what you are teaching him or her?

It should be noted that sometimes you will not need a replacement behavior. For instance, you might be trying to increase the target behavior, such as time on task. In this case, the desired behavior is simply more of the target behavior and not a completely different, or replacement, behavior. Steps for identifying target and replacement behaviors for your child are discussed in chapter 3.

STEP 2: COLLECTING BASELINE DATA AND DETERMINING THE CAUSE OF THE TARGET BEHAVIOR

After you have defined what it is that you want to change about your child, you must then try to figure out why your child displays the behavior that you want to change. This isn't very easy, but it is extremely important. Here is an example.

Imagine that your child is not participating in class and is staring off into space most of the day. Take a few minutes to brainstorm 10 different causes for this behavior. Use the lines below to write down your answers.

_____

_____

_____

What did you come up with? The possibilities are endless, but following are some potential causes for a student to be staring into space:

1. She is "in love."
2. She is on drugs or has been drinking.
3. She has attention deficit hyperactivity disorder (ADHD).
4. She is having petit mal or absence seizures.
5. She is bored in class because she is gifted and the material is too easy for her.
6. She is bored in class because she is lost and doesn't know what is happening.
7. She is trying to upset the teacher or her parents.
8. She is depressed.
9. She is schizophrenic and sees things that are not there.
10. She is tired.

Clearly each of these situations could cause your child to stare off into space. However, you would have to address each behavior differently. For example, if your child is tired, you might have her go to bed earlier or limit her activity on school nights. But if she is depressed, you might have her see a counselor or take antidepressants.

Now imagine that you thought that your child was tired, but she really was depressed. Do you think that sending her to bed earlier or limiting her nighttime activities would help her? Are you starting to see how important determining the cause of the target behavior is? Just think what might happen if your hypothesis was wrong! Your daughter might become more depressed or try to kill herself. For this reason, the importance of identifying the cause of the target behavior cannot be overstated. Determining the cause of the behavior is done by collecting baseline data, discussed in chapter 4.

STEP 3: DEVELOPING AN INTERVENTION TO INCREASE APPROPRIATE BEHAVIOR

Now we get to the bottom line. How do you increase the desired behavior? Generally, you reward behavior that you want to increase. What is considered a reward? How do you develop effective strategies for accomplishing your goals? These questions are addressed in chapter 5.

STEP 4: DEVELOPING AN INTERVENTION TO DECREASE INAPPROPRIATE BEHAVIOR

Whereas reinforcers are used to increase appropriate behaviors, punishers are used to decrease inappropriate behaviors. There are many different methods for reducing behaviors. Chapter 6 will help you find the one that matches your needs and philosophy.

STEP 5: IMPLEMENTING AND EVALUATING THE INTERVENTION

The next step that we address in this book is implementing the programs that you develop and seeing whether they are working. How do you do this? Basically, you compare the behavior that occurred prior to your intervention to your goal. This is why it is necessary to be able to define the behavior in measurable and observable terms. Otherwise, you will never really know if your efforts are successful. We discuss how to evaluate behavior in chapter 7.

Another important issue to consider is what you would consider a successful effort. In other words, how much change does there have to be for your child to achieve the goal? Think about it. Suppose that your child runs in the house or talks too loud. Certainly, you would probably want to decrease these behaviors, but should you really expect that the child will *never* talk too loud or run in the house? The question becomes, is perfect behavior really possible? Are you just setting yourself and your child up for failure?

But what if your child is violent or unsafe? Perhaps he plays with fire or crosses the street without looking. Wouldn't you then want to eliminate the target behavior totally? There is a very fine line between setting realistic goals and setting your expectations so high that your child is doomed to fail before you even begin.

STEP 6: IMPLEMENTING NEW STRATEGIES IF NEEDED

Let's suppose that you have gone through all of the steps that we have outlined. You identified the target and replacement behaviors and defined them in measurable terms. You developed a plan to increase the replacement behavior while decreasing the target behavior. However, when you assess your strategies, you find that nothing is happening. Or worse, you find that the target behavior is actually increasing in frequency or severity. What do you do?

The first step is to figure out why the strategies didn't work. There could be several reasons for this outcome. Perhaps from your child's perspective your reinforcements for the replacement behavior are actually punishments. Or the child gets more from performing the target behavior than he or she loses from punishment. Ideas for strategies are included in chapters 8 and 9.

APPLYING WHAT YOU HAVE LEARNED

By now you have a good grasp of the process that this book follows. Let's see if you can apply what you have learned. Go back to the beginning of the chapter and re-read the case study on Katie Pearson. Then try to answer the questions about the case study. We discuss the questions below.

Question 1: What Is the Target Behavior
That Mrs. Pearson Is Focusing On?

One of the first steps in developing an effective behavioral modification plan is to identify the target behavior, or the behavior that you wish to change. Without a clearly defined target behavior, it becomes difficult to determine whether your plan has had any effect. Look back at the case study. What target behavior did Mrs. Pearson want to change?

Clearly, the behavior that Mrs. Pearson was most concerned about is Katie's destruction of property. Specifically, Katie keeps breaking things that do not belong to her. This would be a good target behavior because it is observable and measurable. Each day, Mrs. Pearson could count the number of things that Katie has broken. So she will be able to take baseline data, implement a strategy, and then see if the behavior has decreased.

Question 2: According to Mrs. Pearson, Why
Is Katie Performing the Target Behavior?

Understanding why people do the things they do is not an easy task. However, it is an extremely important step in trying to improve people's behavior. Without understanding why the behavior is occurring, it is very difficult to change it. According to Mrs. Pearson, why is Katie performing the target behavior? Why is she breaking things?

Mrs. Pearson apparently feels that Katie is breaking things on purpose. If this is the case, then Mrs. Pearson's approach (making Katie pay for the objects that she breaks) might reduce the behavior. However, it should be noted that Mrs. Pearson came to this hypothesis rather quickly. Further, she doesn't have any real evidence to suggest that her daughter is willfully breaking everything.

As we discuss in chapter 4, you will need to collect data on your child before you can successfully determine why the behavior is occurring. These data will not only help you figure out how to change the behavior, but they also will be used to see if you are having the desired effect.

Question 3: Other Than Willful Choice on Her Part, What Other Causes Could Explain Katie's Behavior?

Behaviors can be caused by a multitude of diverse factors. For example, the environment can cause people to behave the way they do. So can biological variables. Other than willful choice, what causes could explain Katie's behavior?

Certainly there are many possibilities as to why Katie is dropping things. For example, perhaps the glasses were wet, which caused her to lose her grip. Or maybe she is experiencing the beginning stages of muscular dystrophy, which is causing a progressive weakness in her hands. In either of these cases, making Katie pay for what she breaks will not change her behavior.

3

STEP 1: IDENTIFYING THE TARGET AND REPLACEMENT BEHAVIORS

CHAPTER OBJECTIVES

By the time you complete this chapter, you should be able to:

- Brainstorm a list of your child's behaviors that you would like to change.
- Prioritize the behaviors that you would like to change.
- Identify potential strategies that could be made to accommodate your child's behavior.
- Consider potential ethical conflicts associated with changing your child's behavior.
- Select specific behaviors that you would like your child to increase or decrease.
- Develop a behavioral objective upon which your behavioral modification plan will be based.

CASE STUDY OF MICHAEL HO

Michael Ho is a student enrolled in a middle school special education program. At the beginning of each school year, Michael's parents and teachers get together to discuss their plans for the coming year. Specifically, they attempt to determine what behaviors they want to teach him. They begin this process by brainstorming a list of the positive behaviors that Michael already has, and then they brainstorm a list of behaviors they would like to see Michael change.

"I, personally, think that Michael is very creative and sweet," his social studies teacher said.

"And a hard worker," added Michael's mathematics teacher. "He always give 110%."

"He is also very caring," Michael's father said, getting a nod of agreement from the rest of the people around the table. "He always worries about how others are doing."

"Actually that is a good transition to our next topic," Michael's special education teacher observed. "What are some of the behaviors that we would like him to change? I for one would like to have him worry less about other people and focus on his own work."

"I agree. He can be a little too social, if you know what I mean. He is frequently out of his desk when he should be completing his assignments."

"Then this year we will focus on getting Michael not to worry about other people so much," Michael's special education teacher said and then paused. "But how should we write that up into a behavioral objective?"

"How about, 'When in class, Michael will worry only about his own affairs'?" somebody suggested.

CASE STUDY QUESTIONS

After reading the case study and this chapter, you should be able to answer the following questions. We will return to the case study and discuss these questions at the end of the chapter.

Question 1: When identifying the target and replacement behaviors, what steps did Michael's teachers and parents forget?

Question 2: What are some of the ethical concerns that might arise when working with Michael on the target behavior?

Question 3: What is wrong with the behavioral objective that is proposed?

INTRODUCTION

As discussed in chapters 1 and 2, the target behavior is the behavior that you are trying to change. For instance, you might want your child to stop hitting other children. Hitting would be the target behavior because it is what you want to decrease.

The replacement behavior is the behavior that you would like to see your child performing. For instance, rather than hitting, you would like your child to explain verbally that she is angry. Talking is the replacement for the hitting.

Sometimes you will not need a replacement behavior since your target behavior might be what you want your child to do. For example, suppose you want your child to increase the time that she exercises. Perhaps she has some potential health issues and needs to complete so many hours of physical therapy. Now, you could say that you want to decrease the time your daughter sits in front of the television, which would be the target behavior, and increase the amount of time she exercises, which would be the replacement behavior.

As we also discussed in chapters 1 and 2, it is very important that you understand why you are focusing on these behaviors. After all, there are many ethical dilemmas when trying to change somebody's behavior. Imagine teaching your child a behavior that actually is damaging to his future! For instance, suppose that your child constantly tells on other children, so you develop a very successful program that changes this behavior. Unfortunately, now your child doesn't tell on people who are doing dangerous or illegal activities.

In addition to considering why you are attempting to change your child's behavior, you must also be able to define the behaviors in such a way that you can accurately measure them. If you can't measure the behaviors, you will not be able to determine whether you are making a positive difference.

In this chapter we outline the steps you will need to take to determine what behaviors you want to focus on. Throughout this chapter there is room for you to write down your thoughts and ideas. Please do not skip over these sections. Brainstorming and self-reflection is a key part of the behavioral modification process. Without completing these activities, you may limit your chances of successfully improving your child's behavior.

STEP 1.1: BRAINSTORMING BEHAVIORS

The first step to identifying the target and replacement behaviors on which you will focus is to brainstorm a list of potential behaviors that might fit the bill. Although you probably can identify a dozen things that annoy you about your child, and even more things that you would like to see your child do, it is really important to go through the brainstorming process and actually think about your child's behavior. After all, what you are about to undertake can be extremely important to your child's future.

Ideal Behaviors

Get a writing implement out. Now close your eyes and think about how you want your child to behave in the ideal world. If you could wave a magic wand and have your child perform any behavior that you wanted, what would you have her do? Would you have your daughter smile more or talk less on the phone, your son pick up his dirty laundry or be better at school?

In the lines below, jot down whatever came to mind. You don't have to write sentences or paragraphs, just a few words or phrases—anything to get the ball rolling. There are no "correct" answers, so just write down whatever comes to mind.

_____

_____

_____

Potential Target Behaviors

Now close your eyes again and think about your child's behaviors that you feel are problematic. These are the behaviors that you might want to change. Maybe he talks back, or she doesn't clean her room, or he doesn't complete his household chores. Again, there are no wrong or right answers.

When you are ready, take some time to write down whatever comes to mind in the lines below. Don't feel bad if you come up with a lot of ideas. This doesn't imply that you are being mean or that your child is a bad kid. You are just brainstorming a list of places that you might want to start. The more ideas you develop, the better off you will be later on.

_____

_____

_____

Good Behaviors That Your Child Does

Hopefully by now you have a few things written down, both in terms of what you want your child to be like in the ideal world as well as areas that could use some improving. You might return to the boxes above as new ideas come to you. You might also need more room, so feel free to write in the margins or on separate pieces of paper. The more you think about your child and what you really want, the better off you will be.

Close your eyes one last time. Think about all of the wonderful things that your child does. Maybe he is very kind and sensitive. Maybe she tries very hard on her schoolwork. Maybe he made you a homemade card for your birthday. It could be anything. There are probably hundreds of things that come to mind. Take a few minutes to write down as many of these things in the box below as you can. Notice that the box provided is twice as large as the other boxes that we used before. This is so that you can try to come up with twice as many good things as you did when you were thinking of problematic behaviors.

_____

_____

_____

_____

_____

_____

It is essential not to lose sight of all the great things that your child does. After all, even Dennis the Menace had his good points, though we might forget them from time to time! So really take time to think of all the things that your child does that make you proud or happy. It could be something as simple as that he picked up his clothes without being told the other day, or that she asked a really insightful question during dinner last week.

When you are done, show this list to your child. In fact, show it to him often, especially after an argument. Maybe put it on the refrigerator door or someplace where your child can see it. Sometimes all children hear is the negative stuff, even though you may think that you are being positive. Reminding them of the great things they do could do wonders in improving their behavior and outlook on life! In addition, update the list regularly and review it whenever you get angry at your child.

You might also want to tell your child why you are reading this book. Explain that you love her and want to help her be even better than she already is. Be honest. Tell her about how you would like her to behave and about the behaviors that you find troublesome. You probably have done this before, but it was most likely right after or during a fight, in which case your child probably had already stopped listening to you.

Now is the perfect time to sit down and have a sincere talk with your child about his or her behavior and your expectations. Talk with your child in a neutral, nonthreatening environment. Maybe take him out to dinner or for ice cream. And don't just focus on the bad stuff, either! Keep stressing the positives that you listed above.

This would be a great time to ask your child to complete the same steps that you have just taken. If your child has the ability, give her a piece of paper and have her write down how she would like to act, what she would like to change about herself, and some of the good things that she does. Maybe have her keep a journal in which she can frequently update and refer back to these lists.

Allowing your child to participate in the process that we are outlining in this book will help you better understand why he is behaving the way he does. Plus, it will give you valuable insight as to who your child is and what is on his mind. If your child is very young or has a cognitive disability, you might have to help him a little more. Perhaps, instead of writing the lists, he can simply talk to you about his perceptions. You might be surprised what you will learn.

STEP 1.2: PRIORITIZING

Okay, so now you have three lists. One focuses on the behavior that you would ideally like to see your child performing. The second contains the behaviors that you would like to change in some way. The third, and perhaps most important if not the longest, is the list of the many good things that your child does. Now what?

Chances are you developed quite a list of behaviors to change. You probably also wrote down a lot of behaviors that you would like to see your child learn. Unfortunately, you only have so many hours a day, and your child can only learn so much in any given time, so you will need to prioritize your goals.

List in Order of Importance

One way to prioritize your goals is to list them in order of importance. This is more difficult than it sounds. After all, which is more important, doing well in school or having a lot of friends? Both are very important for your child's future and happiness, but which would you focus on first? Following are some activities that might help you decide.

Ideal behaviors. Go back to the first group of lines and take a few minutes to look at the list of new behaviors that you would like to see your child display. Consider each one in turn. Lightly cross out the ones that really aren't that important. For example, maybe upon further reflection you really don't care if your child uses "who" and "whom" correctly—after all, most adults don't nowadays.

Now circle the behaviors that you think are absolutely essential for your child to live a happy, healthy, and productive life. If you have circled more than two or three, you will need to determine which is the most important and which you will focus on later. Use the following box to help you put them in the proper order of importance (1 being the most important of the behaviors).

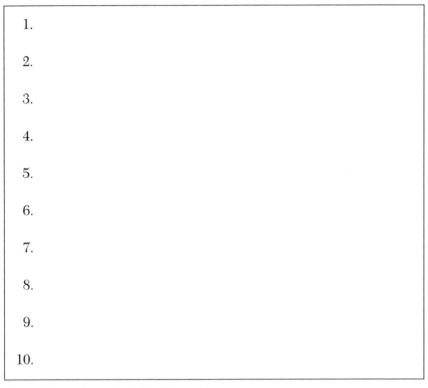

1.

2.

3.

4.

5.

6.

7.

8.

9.

10.

Box 3.1   Most Important Ideal Behaviors

Problematic behaviors.   Now do the same thing with the problematic behaviors. Look at the list that you created in the second group of lines. Cross out any that you no longer think are relevant. Then circle the ones that are very important and must be addressed.

Take a few minutes to look at what you circled. Then ask yourself, "Why are these particular behaviors important?" It is important for you to reflect on how important these behaviors are to you. After thinking about it for a few minutes, you might say to yourself, "Hey, my kid isn't so bad! Sure he runs in the house once in a while, but I can live with that." You also might learn something about your own expectations and values. Maybe the behaviors are only problematic because they get on your nerves and are really not *that* important after all.

In the box below list the behaviors in order of their importance, 1 being the most crucial.

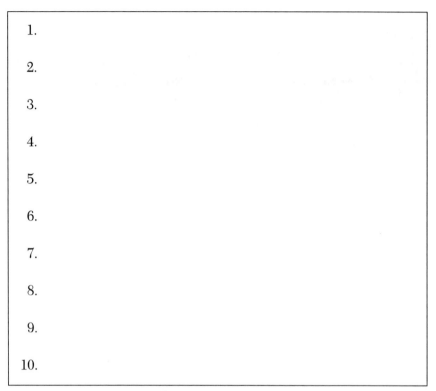

1.

2.

3.

4.

5.

6.

7.

8.

9.

10.

Box 3.2   Most Important Problematic Behaviors

Mutually Inclusive Behaviors

Look at the behaviors that you just prioritized. Are there any that overlap or affect each other? For example, maybe you want your child to stop yelling at her sister (problematic behavior) and you want your children to play nicely together (ideal behavior). These behaviors complement each other. That is, if you decrease the yelling, you might be able to increase the appropriate playing.

Look again at your lists in the boxes. Are there any behaviors that might be causing other behaviors? For example, maybe your child frequently gets out of his chair and hits other children. If you could teach him to sit in his chair, he won't be able to hit the other students (assuming that they don't sit too close to each other).

In the following two-column box, rewrite the behaviors that you prioritized. Then draw lines connecting the behaviors that you think are linked. If you see that several behaviors are connected, these may be the ones you should address first.

Ideal Behaviors	Problematic Behaviors
1.	1.
2.	2.
3.	3.
4.	4.
5.	5.
6.	6.
7.	7.
8.	8.
9.	9.
10.	10.

Box 3.3   Links Between Ideal Behavior and Problematic Behavior

Difficulty of Success

Some of the behaviors that you listed might be easy to learn or to change. For example, maybe your child already is able to sit still for 10 minutes and, with a little prompting, she should be able to increase that time to 12 or 15 minutes. Or maybe your child hits himself an average of 200 times a day. Cutting that to 0 may take some time and a lot of hard work.

However, just because it will take a long time doesn't mean that you shouldn't attempt to modify a certain behavior. Obviously, behaviors that are unsafe, such as running into traffic, need to be addressed regardless of the effort required. Still, if there are no absolutely urgent behaviors to concentrate on, you might want to start with the easiest behaviors and then build on your child's success. After all, once the child sees that she can achieve something, maybe the harder behaviors will be easier to manage.

Take a few minutes to consider the ideal and problematic behaviors that you listed in the last box. Which would be the most difficult for your child to learn? Which would be the easiest? In the box below, prioritize each group of behaviors from easiest (1) to hardest (10) to achieve.

Ideal Behaviors	Problematic Behaviors
1.	1.
2.	2.
3.	3.
4.	4.
5.	5.
6.	6.
7.	7.
8.	8.
9.	9.
10.	10.

Box 3.4   Ideal Behavior and Problematic Behavior by Level of Difficulty to Achieve

Resources Needed

In addition to the level of difficulty, you should consider whether teaching your child a particular behavior is going to require any specialized resources. For instance, if your child has profound mental retardation and you want to teach him how to communicate more effectively, you might require a computerized communication device. Or if your child has a physical disability and you want him to be able to get around the house independently, you might have to purchase a wheelchair or arm braces. If the resources that you need are not currently available to you, you might have to focus on a different behavior—at least until the resources become available.

In the following two-column box, list the ideal and problematic behaviors. Below each behavior, write any resources that you may need to address that specific behavior. The resources can be as general as "need help from grandparents on weekends" or as specific as "need Math Master 2000 computer program."

Ideal Behaviors	Problematic Behaviors
Behavior #1:	Behavior #1:
Resources Needed:	Resources Needed:
Behavior #2:	Behavior #2:
Resources Needed:	Resources Needed:
Behavior #3:	Behavior #3:
Resources Needed:	Resources Needed:
Behavior #4:	Behavior #4:
Resources Needed:	Resources Needed:
Behavior #5:	Behavior #5:
Resources Needed:	Resources Needed:
Behavior #6:	Behavior #6:
Resources Needed:	Resources Needed:

Box 3.5   Resources Needed for Addressing Ideal Behavior and Problematic Behavior

Box 3.5 *(Continued)*

Behavior #7	Behavior #7
Resources Needed:	Resources Needed:
Behavior #8	Behavior #8
Resources Needed:	Resources Needed:
Behavior #9	Behavior #9
Resources Needed:	Resources Needed:
Behavior #10	Behavior #10
Resources Needed:	Resources Needed:

STEP 1.3: ACCOMMODATIONS, ETHICS, AND OTHER CONSIDERATIONS

By now you should have your target and replacement behaviors selected. Before we go on, it is important for you to consider several things, including why these behaviors are important to change as well as methods for accommodating the behaviors. This is your "final check" to see whether you really want to go through with addressing these behaviors, so please consider these issues carefully.

Accommodations

Often the behaviors that parents and teachers want to change are not the result of a willful desire on the child's part but are due to a disability or some biological condition, such as normal development. For example, imagine that your child stares off into space and doesn't pay attention whenever you are talking to her. Would this be a behavior that you would try to change? Probably, especially if your child was doing this willfully. But what if she had attention deficit hyperactivity disorder (ADHD)? What if she had epilepsy and was having petit mal seizures (also called absence seizures)? What if she had a hearing problem, or autism? Would you still try to modify her behavior even if it was caused by something biological?

The point is, sometimes it is better to make accommodations for behavior rather than trying to change it. For example, instead of punishing your child every time she doesn't pay attention or rewarding her whenever she is, perhaps it is easier and better if you accept her behavior and try minimize it by other means, such as by making sure that you have her attention before you start talking to her and keeping dialogues short and to the point. You might also change the environment. Moving the child to the front of the class or putting a rug on the floor to dampen noise might help her concentrate.

Although there are behaviors that certainly need to be accommodated, disabilities shouldn't be an excuse to misbehave. A student with ADHD should not be expected to sit still for three hours straight, yet students should not be allowed to use ADHD as an excuse for disrupting their classmates. So where do you draw the line? When do you accommodate behavior, and when do you try to change it?

In the end, you are going to have to decide what to do. However, following are some questions to help you determine whether to accommodate a behavior or try to change it. Take time to consider each carefully.

The changeability of the behavior. The first thing that you probably should ask yourself is, "Can the behavior be changed?" If it cannot, then everything else is moot. For example, a child who has epilepsy cannot control whether she has a petit mal seizure and stares off into space for a few seconds. Likewise, a child who has Tourrette's syndrome cannot always control his vocal tics.

Unfortunately, there is a great deal of gray area surrounding other conditions. For instance, many students with ADHD can stop fidgeting or pay attention for at least a short while. Students with dyslexia can read fine at times and not at all at others. Knowing when your child is not doing what she is supposed to because of a disability rather than because she is unwilling is very important but often very difficult. This is where knowing your child comes in handy.

The integrity of your child. The next thing that you should ask yourself is, "Would my child use his condition to his benefit?" In other words, would he fake having a seizure or use ADHD as an excuse to misbehave? Think about it. If your child said that she was sick and couldn't go to school today, would you believe her? If he did something bad, would he 'fess up to what he had done? If you asked her whether she did something on purpose, would she tell you the truth?

Only you can answer these questions. You probably know your child better than anybody. If you think that your child could be using a disability as cover for his willful misbehaviors, don't feel bad. It is only natural for kids to fib now and again. This doesn't make your child a juvenile delinquent. Still, it might make you question whether his behavior is really preventable.

Look at the behaviors that you indicated you want to change. Are there any that could be out of your child's control? Maybe the behaviors are caused by a disability, or perhaps they are the result of the child's maturity level. In the box on the next page (box 3.6), indicate in the left-hand column the potential target behaviors that you brainstormed that might need to be accommodated, rather than changed.

Next try to think of some ways that you can address the behavior without actually trying to change your child. Are there things that you could do that would reduce the behavior? Maybe you could change the environment or how you react when the behavior occurs. Jot down your ideas for potential accommodations in the right-hand column.

Ignoring Behaviors

Another question that you have to ask yourself before you go any further is, "Will the target behaviors go away without any interventions?" In other words, if you just ignore them, will they stop occurring? Chances are you have already tried this, but if not, you might want to. But then again, there are some behaviors you simply cannot ignore, such as those that are violent or dangerous.

Ethical Considerations

A final question you need to ask yourself before you move on: "Why do I want to change my child's behavior?" Are you attempting to change the behavior simply to preserve your sanity? Will changing your child's

Behaviors	Accommodations for Each Behavior
Example Behavior: Not paying attention	Example Accommodations: Remove distractions, be brief when presenting information, make sure the child is paying attention by asking questions, move to the front of the room, make the environment quieter.

Box 3.6   Behaviors That Might Require Accommodations

behavior help prepare her for the future? Will your child be better off performing the replacement behavior? Is there a high degree of likelihood that your child is going to learn how to do the replacement behavior?

In chapter 1 we discussed the ethical factors that are involved with behavioral modification. This is your last chance to really sit down and decide whether it is appropriate for you to change your child's behavior. Please don't undertake this task without really thinking about what you want to accomplish. The decisions that you make may affect your child for the rest of his life.

STEP 1.4: SELECTING BEHAVIORS

Thus far you have prioritized the various behaviors that you want to replace (i.e., the "problematic behaviors") and the behaviors that you want to replace them with (i.e., the "ideal behaviors). You have looked at which behaviors are the most important, which are linked to other behaviors, which would be the easiest to teach, and so forth. Now you will need to figure out what specifically you are going to address.

Unfortunately there is no magic way of determining what to focus on first. In the end, you will have to rely on your gut feelings. What do you think should be the first behaviors you should change? Only you know your child and what kind of time you have to spend working on this endeavor. There are, however, some tips that might make it easier for you to decide:

- Focus on changing only one or two behaviors at a time.
- If you focus on changing multiple behaviors, address behaviors that are related (e.g., "in-house behaviors," such as no running inside and no yelling inside).
- If this is your first time developing behavioral modification programs, start off simple.
- If your child is easily frustrated or defiant, start off focusing on something that is likely to succeed.

Take a deep breath. Look at all the information you have written down. Now try to identify one or two of your child's behaviors that you would like to change. Throughout the rest of this book, we will refer to these as your "target behaviors." In the appropriate space provided in the two-column box below, write the target behaviors down. Also think about the behaviors with which you want to replace the target behaviors.

These are the "ideal" behaviors that you want your child to perform. Throughout the rest of the book, we will call these your "replacement behaviors." Write these down in the right-hand column. We will come back to them frequently, so make sure these are the behaviors that you want to address.

Target Behavior(s)	Replacement Behavior(s)
1.	1.
2.	2.

Box 3.7   Your Target and Replacement Behaviors

STEP 1.5: FINE TUNING THE TARGET AND REPLACEMENT BEHAVIORS

Take a look at the one or two target and replacement behaviors on which you have decided to focus (see the box above). If you have not already done so, you will need to break down the behaviors into very concrete, observable actions. For example, let's suppose that you want to increase your child's organizational skills. That's good. Effective organizational skills will really help your child in many ways. But what do you really mean by "organizational skills?" What *exactly* do you want your child to do? Think about it. Organizational skills can be broken into many specific behaviors, including (but certainly not limited to):

- Writing down due dates for assignments on a calendar.
- Keeping work areas (e.g., desk) clean.
- Putting homework in the proper folders.
- Bringing home all materials needed to complete homework.

So rather than focusing on broad behaviors, try breaking your goals into manageable steps, or smaller behaviors. In the next box, write down the target and replacement behaviors that you come up with after prioritizing the list that you brainstormed. Now take a moment to think about what specific behaviors you want to work on. When you are ready, write down the steps for each of the original behaviors. These smaller steps are what you will be addressing throughout the rest of the book.

Target Behavior #1 Specific Observable Behaviors:	Replacement Behavior #1: Specific Observable Behaviors:

Target Behavior #2
  (if applicable):
 	
Specific Observable Behaviors:
	Replacement Behavior #2
	  (if applicable):
	
	Specific Observable Behaviors:

Box 3.8   Specific Behaviors upon Which You Will Be Focusing

STEP 1.6: CREATING BEHAVIORAL OBJECTIVES

Hopefully the previous information has helped you narrow down what you want to do to help your child. If this is your first time formally using behavioral modification, you might want to start with only one target behavior and one replacement behavior. Later, as you get more practice, you could try to modify several behaviors at once.

Now that you have an objective or two, it is time to write them down in measurable terms. As discussed previously, it is important to write the behaviors down so that you are being consistent throughout the entire process. If you keep changing how you define the behaviors in question, you are likely to confuse your child and have little success.

If you have a child in special education, you will probably recognize behavioral objectives. They are used in individualized education programs (IEPs). Behavioral objectives contain three components:

- Behavior
- Condition
- Criterion

Behavior

When creating behavioral objectives, it is extremely important that the behavior be observable. Otherwise you will not be able to determine whether you and your child are making progress. Further, each objective should only have one behavior. In other words, you will have an objective for each behavior that you are trying to change.

Putting behaviors in measurable terms is a lot more difficult than it sounds. Look at the following examples. Which behaviors are observable?

1. Being out-of-seat
2. Being impolite
3. Not listening when spoken to
4. Hitting other people
5. Annoying people

Of the five behaviors listed, only numbers 1 (being out-of-seat) and 4 (hitting other people) are measurable. You can see if a child is out of his seat or if he is hitting somebody. Being impolite is very subjective. What you might consider impolite or annoying, another person might consider being assertive or funny. Further, how can you tell if your child is listening to you? Sure, she can be looking at you and nodding her head, she can even repeat what you just said word-for-word, but does that really mean she is listening?

In the lines below, try writing down the target behavior in measurable terms. Remember, it should be written so that everybody watching the behavior would agree that it occurred or did not occur.

_____

_____

_____

Condition

The condition states when the behavior will occur. It usually is a dependent clause at the beginning of the objective. For example, "When instructed by the teacher or parent, Jimmy will sit in his chair," or "When given homework by her teacher, Sara will finish the assignments." In these examples, the conditions are "when instructed by the teacher or parent" and "when given homework." Sitting in his chair and finishing the assignments are measurable behaviors. Without conditions, it sounds as though Jimmy has to sit in his chair all of the time!

In the following lines, write down your measurable behaviors with their conditions.

_____

_____

_____

Criterion

The criterion is how you know if your child has achieved the objective. In other words, this is the degree to which the behavior has to occur for you to be happy. It is usually a dependent clause at the end of the objective. For example, a behavioral objective might be, "When instructed by the teacher or parent, Jimmy will sit in his chair for five minutes," or "When given homework by her teacher, Sara will finish the assignments with 80 percent accuracy." The clauses "for five minutes" and "with 80 percent accuracy" are the criteria against which the child's behavior is measured.

In the lines below, write the behavioral objectives for each of the behaviors that you want your child to work on. Remember, the condition (e.g., when the behavior is to occur) goes first. Then comes one measurable behavior. Finally, write the criterion (e.g., to what degree or how frequently you want the behavior performed). This will be your behavioral objective. We will be referring back to it throughout the entire book.

_____

_____

_____

APPLYING WHAT YOU HAVE LEARNED

By now you have a clear understanding of how to identify an appropriate target and replacement behavior for your child (see figure 3.1). Let's apply what you have learned in this chapter to the case study. Go back to the beginning of the chapter and re-read the case study about Michael Ho. Then try to answer the case study questions.

Question 1: When Identifying the Target and Replacement Behaviors, What Steps Did Michael's Teachers and Parents Forget?

It is essential to follow the steps that are outlined in these chapters. Failure to do so might prevent you from developing an effective behavioral modification plan. For example, if you forget to brainstorm potential target behaviors, you might not address a key issue that could help your child live a happy and productive life.

Take a look at what was done in the case study. You have a whole bunch of people gathered together trying to help Michael. When identifying appropriate target and replacement behaviors, do they follow all the steps outlined in this chapter? Which steps do they forget? Why are these steps important?

The team did brainstorm a list of positive behaviors that Michael does and behaviors that they would like to see changed. However, this process seems a bit rushed. It was almost as if they only thought of a couple potential target behaviors before they moved on. They might have benefited from further discussion and additional consideration.

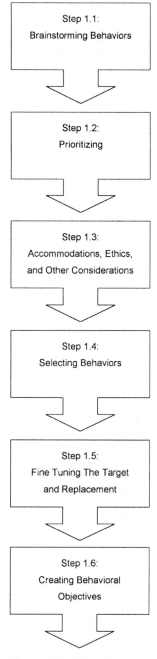

Figure 3.1   Flow Chart of Step 1

Unfortunately, the group never prioritized the target behaviors they identified. Because they did not think about what behaviors are most pressing, they could be focusing on a behavior that is less important than something else. For instance, maybe working on Michael's self-esteem is far more important than the fact that he likes talking to other students. Without adequately brainstorming ideas and then prioritizing what you come up with, it is very difficult to develop effective plans.

The group also did not identify replacement behaviors to teach Michael. Basically, this is the equivalent of saying to Michael, "Don't do that!" It is okay to tell him what not to do, but they should also tell him what behavior he should be doing instead.

Question 2: What Are Some of the Ethical Concerns That Might Arise When Working with Michael on the Target Behavior?

As discussed in previous chapters, modifying people's behavior is filled with potential ethical dilemmas. For example, the target behavior that you may be trying to reduce might actually be appropriate in some settings. So, if you extinguish that behavior, your child might not be able to function appropriately in those settings.

Think about Michael and what his teachers and parents are trying to do. Are there any ethical issues that they should consider before proceeding? What are they?

The target behavior that the team has identified for Michael involves caring about other people's business. Yes, there are times when people should keep their noses to themselves and not butt into other people's private affairs. However, there are also times when it is very good and appropriate to worry about other people. By working on this target behavior, the group runs the risk of making Michael antisocial and uncaring. Is that what they really want? Or do they simply want him to stay seated during class time?

Question 3: What Is Wrong with the Behavioral Objective That Is Proposed?

Developing formal behavioral objectives will help you to clarify exactly what you want your child to do and when you want him to do it.

They also help you determine whether your child has succeeded in changing. Without good behavioral objectives, it is difficult to effectively change people's behavior.

Look at the behavioral objective that somebody proposed for Michael. Now go back and look at how to write beneficial behavioral objectives. What is wrong with what they proposed?

There are so many things wrong with the proposed objective that it is difficult to know where to begin. First of all, they do have a condition, "When in class . . . ." Conditions tell you when or where the behavior is expected to occur. Unfortunately, the behavior is far from being measurable. How could you determine whether Michael is worrying about his own affairs? Finally, there is no criterion. Without a criterion, you can't tell if Michael has achieved his goal.

STEP 2: COLLECTING BASELINE DATA AND DETERMINING THE CAUSE OF THE TARGET BEHAVIOR

CHAPTER OBJECTIVES

By the time you complete this chapter, you should be able to:

- Identify times and places when data should be collected regarding your child's behavior.
- Determine methods for collecting data on your child's behavior based on the strengths and weaknesses of the data collection methods as well as the needs of your child.
- Collect data on your child's behavior.
- Analyze the data collected to determine the function of your child's behavior.

CASE STUDY OF AHIB SALIZAR

Ahib had always behaved himself at school. Ever since he was a young child, teachers had commented on what a gentleman he was and how he would go out of his way to help other students. However, after he entered middle school, two of his teachers began sending notes home complaining about his "inappropriate interactions." Ahib's mother simply could not understand what had caused the change.

"I don't understand it," Ahib's mother said to a friend on the phone. "He has always been very good at school. I can't imagine why he is acting like this."

"Well, let's look at this scientifically," the friend suggested. "What exactly is Ahib doing that is so bad?"

"Apparently he keeps talking to his classmates when the teacher is trying to lecture."

"Is he doing this in all of his classes?"

"No. It is just in English and Social Studies. I have talked to all of his other teachers and he apparently is acting fine for them."

"So how are these two teachers different than the rest of his teachers?" the friend asked, adding, "Are they female? Young? Old? Mean?"

Ahib's mother thought for a moment, trying to find a common link between the two teachers. "They are both men," she said. "But I don't think that is it. He has other male teachers and he is wonderful in their classes. And I don't think their age has anything to do with it, either. One is pretty young . . . in his twenties. The other is probably closer to his late forties."

"Does he sit in the back of the room in the two classes and in the front for everybody else? Maybe sitting in the back gives him more of an opportunity to chitchat with his friends."

"You know, I thought of that. I even suggested to one of the teachers that he should move Ahib to the front of the room, but he is already sitting there in that class. In the second class, he is sitting kind of to the side in the middle."

"Are there certain days when he is more talkative than others? Like on Mondays? Maybe he simply wants to tell his friends what he did all weekend."

"I don't think so. The notes are sent home pretty regularly."

"What is going on when he is talking? Maybe the teachers were having small group activities and Ahib was still working or something. Or maybe he is bored during the teacher's lectures."

"I don't know. It sounds like it is a pretty constant type of thing. Still, that wouldn't explain why it is only occurring in these two classes."

"True," the friend paused and thought. There was a brief silence. Then she asked, "Who is he talking to? Is it the same person in both classes?"

"Yes! You know, I think he is sitting next to the same person in both classes. I forgot what her name is, but Ahib talks about her a lot!"

"Well, there you go. I bet he likes this girl and feels compelled to talk with her. Maybe you can have the teachers move them apart and see if that fixes the problem."

"That is such a good idea! You know, he is getting to be at that age where girls are beginning to catch his eye. Hopefully this will solve the problem."

STUDY QUESTIONS

Question 1: Why is it important to know when Ahib is acting inappropriately and when he is not?

Question 2: How could Ms. Salizar either confirm or refute her hypothesis regarding the cause of Ahib's behavior?

Question 3: If somebody were to observe Ahib in the two classes, what recording schedules should probably be used?

INTRODUCTION

By now, you should have an idea as to which of your child's behaviors you would like to change. As discussed in previous chapters, we call this the "target behavior." The next step in modifying your child's behavior is to determine why your child is exhibiting the behavior that you want to change.

This step is very important. Imagine for a moment that you are a child and you have trouble sitting still at the dinner table. Your parents yell at you. They offer you your favorite dessert. They even threaten to spank you if you don't stop squirming. But you can't. Why? Because the chair is uncomfortable. Maybe there is a sharp piece of wood poking you! Of course you can't sit still, no matter what your parents do or say!

Consider another example. Suppose that your child always argues with you. You tell him to do his chores and he yells that he won't. You tell him to go to bed and he says that he doesn't have to. You tell him that he has to take a bath and he tells you that he took one yesterday.

You try to reason with your child, but the more you do, the more he argues. Why is he behaving like this? Well, maybe it is because he doesn't want to do his chores, go to bed, or take a bath. Further, the more he argues with you, the more time he wastes and the greater the chances are of not having to do what he doesn't want to do. In other words, your approach to the problem (i.e., reasoning with him) is actually playing right into his hands. He wants you to waste time so he doesn't have to do the things that you are telling him to do.

Now this is not to say that you shouldn't reason with your child. You should. It is a wonderful way to teach and build communication skills and develop a loving relationship. However, you must also consider why the behavior is occurring before you try to change it. That is what this chapter is all about: figuring out why your child is acting the way she does.

STEP 2.1: THINGS TO CONSIDER BEFORE COLLECTING DATA

To determine why your child performs the target behavior, you must gather baseline data. If you remember from chapter 1, baseline describes the target behavior before you attempt to change it. However, prior to gathering data, you must ask yourself several questions.

Time of Day

Think about the behavior that you are trying to change (see the last box in chapter 3). When does it occur? Does it tend to be in the morning on a school day? At night, when your child is tired and has to go to bed? After coming in from playing outside? During the weekend? Your child's behavior probably does not occur randomly. If you take the time to observe, using the following lines as a kind of journal, you might see a pattern to when the behavior manifests itself.

_____

_____

_____

Location

Now try to recall where the behavior occurs. Is it on the playground? At the dinner table? On the school bus? In class? In the hallways in between classes? Again, your child's behavior probably doesn't occur everywhere. More than likely, it is more frequent or intense in a specific location or two. If you can't recall specific places where the behavior occurs, observe your child for several days. Then use the following lines to record where you think the behavior occurs most.

_____

_____

_____

Who Is Nearby?

When you are thinking back to the last few times that the target behavior occurred, try to recall whether anybody else was around. For instance, were there other kids around? Other adults? Teachers? Does the same person or people seem to be around whenever the behavior occurs? In the following lines, write down the people who are around when the behavior occurs.

_____

_____

_____

Antecedents

As discussed briefly in chapter 1, "antecedents" are things that occur right before an event. Chances are, your child's target behavior doesn't just occur randomly. Something probably triggers the behavior. Maybe somebody teases your child. Or your child just lost at a game. Or maybe your child was just told what to do by an adult. Or maybe your child just woke up. It could be anything. Take a minute or two to write down what occurs right before the behavior manifests itself.

_____

_____

_____

Consequences of the Behavior

Now think about what happens after the target behavior occurs. Do other kids laugh? Do adults get angry? Does your child get sent out of the room? Does your child avoid something like eating dinner or being in class? Chances are your child is trying to use her behavior as a way of either getting something or avoiding something. Can you figure out what? Take a few minutes to think about this and then jot down some notes in the lines below.

_____

_____

_____

STEP 2.2: SELECTING METHODS FOR GATHERING DATA

Look at what you have written on the preceding pages. Does anything jump out at you? Is there a pattern or any clues as to why the target behavior is occurring? Maybe there is somebody who is triggering the behavior. Or maybe the behavior only happens at a certain time or in a specific environment. If you can formulate some sort of working hypothesis about what is causing the target behavior, you will be in very good shape.

The next step in determining what is causing the target behavior is to collect data to see whether your hypothesis is correct. If you don't have a clue why the behavior is happening, don't despair. This step might make it a little clearer.

Before you can start collecting data on the target behavior and developing a baseline, you have to figure out how to collect the data. There are many strategies that might help. Try to collect data in a variety of ways. For example, you could observe, interview teachers, and ask your child to collect data on his own behavior. After all, the more ways you have to look at it, the more likely you will solve the mystery.

If you do not have any ideas about why the behavior is occurring, then try to gather data in a number of different environments and times. Maybe you will find that the behavior is occurring in one place more than another. Or maybe the behavior is occurring during a certain period of the day. If you have a good notion as to when or where the behavior occurs, then try to collect data only when the likelihood of the behavior occurring is high.

Examining Existing Data

Perhaps the simplest and least time-consuming method for gathering data on the target behavior is to look at information that already exists. For example, if you want to focus on your child's school attendance or her grades, you need only look at the teacher's attendance sheet or grade book. Why reinvent the wheel?

Self-Reporting

Often it is useful to have your child collect data on her own behavior. For example, suppose that you are trying to determine how often your child does her homework or completes his chores. You could keep a log on the refrigerator door where the child has to check off whether she did what she was supposed to do. Of course, there are a few problems with this approach.

First, no offense, but your child could be lying. In that case your data would not help you much. However, this might give you an idea for another behavior to focus on!

Second, your child maybe unwilling to participate. Or your child might not be able to participate in data collection. This can often be the case if your child is very young or has a disability such as profound mental retardation.

Finally, the act of collecting data might actually change your child's behavior. Think about it this way. Your parents want to measure how often you take the garbage out, so they put a checklist on the refrigerator that you are supposed to mark every time you complete the task. However, the checklist itself is a constant visual reminder that you should do the task, so it is very likely that it will actually increase the target behavior.

Observations

Observing your child is one of the best ways to collect data and attempt to figure out why she is acting the way she is. No matter the target behavior, you probably should take some time to observe your child when the behavior is transpiring, as well as beforehand and afterwards. These observations might help you answer the questions that we covered in Step 2.1. In the next step, we discuss how you can record your observations.

STEP 2.3: SELECTING METHODS FOR RECORDING OBSERVATIONS

Now that you have figured out where and when you plan to observe your child, you will need to figure out how you plan to record what you see. The method of recording observations will often depend on the behavior that you are investigating. Table 4.1 lists several ways of recording data, including:

- anecdotal recording
- frequency recording
- duration recording
- latency recording
- interval recording
- time sampling

Table 4.1   Summary of Methods to Record Observations

Method	Summary
Anecdotal Recording	Recording of general information that you witness during the observation
Frequency Recording	Recording of the exact number of times that the behavior occurs during the observation
Duration Recording	Recording the length of time that the behavior lasted during the observation
Latency Recording	Recording of the length of time between the trigger and when the behavior actually occurred during the observation
Interval Recording	Recording whether or not the behavior occurred at least once during a specific period of time
Time Sample Recording	Recording whether the behavior was occurring exactly at a specific period of time

Anecdotal Recording

One way that you can collect data is simply to take notes about what you see happening. This is called anecdotal recording. Basically, you observe and jot down a description of what you see. For example, you might note how your child appears to look (e.g., "Kris can't seem to concentrate when she has to do her math assignments right when she gets home from school."), or behaviors that you may not have noticed before (e.g., "Robin looks at boys every time one walks by."). You can write anything down that you think may have something to do with the target behavior. The better observer you are, the better this strategy could work.

The problem with anecdotal recording is that it is not very objective or scientific. As a result, it is difficult to compare one day's notes to the next. So you should use anecdotal in conjunction with other data collection procedures.

Frequency Recording

Frequency recording involves measuring behavior each and every time it occurs. For example, suppose that you want to know how many times your child gets out of her seat during class. When using frequency recording, you would observe the child and simply count every time she got up during a set period of time.

Frequency recording is particularly helpful when you are interested in how many times a behavior occurs in given environments or during specific periods of time. However, the target behavior has to have a clear beginning and end point, such as hitting somebody. You can tell exactly how many times your child hit one of his siblings.

It is a little more difficult to use frequency recording with a behavior like talking. Yes, you could count each word that is said, but it would be difficult to count the number of conversations. After all, when does one conversation end and another one start?

In addition, frequency recording would not be appropriate if the behavior occurs so often that you couldn't count it accurately. For instance, imagine that you want to measure how often your child fidgets. So you observe her for 15 minutes and put a tally mark on a piece of paper every time she bounces her knee. Imagine how difficult this would be if she bounced her knees as fast as she could or if she bounced both of her knees at the same time! In this situation, frequency recording would probably not be practical.

Another downside to frequency recording is that it only tells you how often the behavior occurs. It doesn't tell you other information, such as when the specific behavior occurs or whether there is a pattern to the behavior. Look at figure 4.1. What can you tell about the child's behavior? Can you tell when the behavior is occurring? Is the child swearing throughout the day? Or is he having one outburst containing multiple swear words? What words is he saying? Is he mad when he is swearing? Did he hurt himself and then start swearing? All of this is important information that frequency recording does not provide.

Duration Recording

Duration recording measures how long a behavior lasts. This recording method is particularly useful when the target behavior is not problematic because of its frequency but because of the time it consumes. For instance, suppose that you want to measure the length of time your child is on-task doing his homework. Rather than measuring each and every time she is doing her homework (i.e., frequency recording), you could keep track of the amount of time that she spends sitting at her desk.

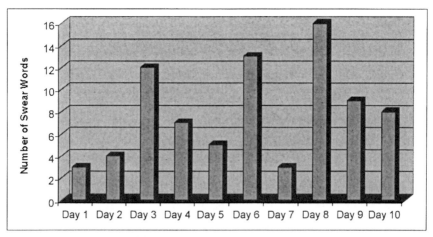

Figure 4.1   Frequency of Swearing

As with frequency recording, duration recording is only beneficial when the target behavior has a clear beginning and end. Further, you shouldn't use duration recording when the behavior occurs so quickly that you can't measure it accurately. Imagine trying to time how long it takes your child to blink! It would be difficult to time each individual event.

Latency Recording

Let's suppose that you have a child who doesn't like doing what he is told. Every time you tell him to do something, such as clean his room, he takes a very long time getting around to it. So the problem is not that he doesn't do what you want or that he takes a long time doing it, he just refuses to do it when you tell him. In other words, you want to decrease the delay between the time you tell him to do something and when he actually starts to do it. In situations such as these, latency recording is the best method of investigation. Latency recording, however, would not be appropriate if you wanted to find out how long a behavior lasted or how frequently it occurred.

Interval Recording

When using event recording, you are measuring each and every behavior that occurs during a certain period. When using duration recording, you measure how long the behavior lasts. With latency recording, you are measuring how long it takes for your child to initiate a behavior after some sort of stimulus, such as being told to pick up her clothes. Interval recording blends many of the characteristics of these other methods.

To use interval recording, you would select a time period (e.g., 30 minutes) and break it up into equal sections, perhaps 30 one-minute intervals. You would then record whether the target behavior occurred during that interval (not the number of times it occurred, just whether it occurred).

To illustrate interval recording, imagine again that you want to measure out-of-seat behavior. Although interval recording does not tell you exactly how many times the behavior occurs, it can provide you with some important information, such as when it occurs. It may also show you if there is a pattern to the behavior (see figure 4.2).

12:00 pm	12:01	12:02	12:03	12:04
	✓	✓	✓	
12:05	12:06	12:07	12:08	12:09
	✓		✓	✓
12:10	12:11	12:12	12:13	12:14
✓				
12:15	12:16	12:17	12:18	12:19
		✓		
12:20	12:21	12:22	12:23	12:24
12:25	12:26	12:27	12:28	12:29

Figure 4.2   An Example of Data Collected Via Interval Recording

Note: Checks indicate that the target behavior occurred at least once in the 1-minute time frame.

Time Sampling

Time sampling is very much like interval recording. With both systems, you break your observation period into equal units. However, with interval recording, you record whether the behavior occurred at any time during that period. With time sampling, you record whether the behavior is occurring exactly as each interval begins.

For instance, suppose that you want to investigate your child talking in class. You would select a time period (e.g., 45 minutes) and divide it into equal intervals (e.g., 30 seconds). At the beginning of every 30-second period, you would indicate whether he was talking.

Note that you cannot tell how many times the child has actually talked. Nor can you say for sure whether he was talking continuously over multiple periods or whether he just happened to make a brief comment right at the beginning of each interval. Time sampling, however, does give you a general feel for when the behavior is occurring and its duration or frequency (see figure 4.3).

12:00 pm	12:01	12:02	12:03	12:04
	✓		✓	
12:05	12:06	12:07	12:08	12:09
				✓
12:10	12:11	12:12	12:13	12:14
✓				
12:15	12:16	12:17	12:18	12:19
		✓		
12:20	12:21	12:22	12:23	12:24
12:25	12:26	12:27	12:28	12:29

Figure 4.3 An Example of Data Collected Via Time Sampling

Note: Checks indicate that the target behavior occurred exactly at the time identified in the box.

STEP 2.4: COLLECTING DATA

Okay, now that you have selected a variety of different ways to measure the target behavior, it is time to begin collecting information. There are some tips to keep in mind.

Secrecy

Perhaps the most important thing to keep in mind when gathering data on your children's behavior is to make sure that they don't know that you are monitoring their behavior. If your children realize that they are being evaluated, they are more apt to act differently than they normally do. This just makes sense. So, when observing, try not to look like you are taking notes or keeping track of anything in particular.

Keep It Simple

Data collection doesn't have to be a complex procedure. In fact, the simpler the better. For example, if you are using a frequency recording system, you might put a bunch of pennies in your left pocket. Then, when you see the behavior, you nonchalantly transfer one penny from the left pocket to the right one. At the end of the observation period, all you have to do is count how many pennies you have in the right pocket and you can determine the behavior's frequency. A little creativity can go a long way.

Gather Data When the Behavior Is Likely to Occur

Let's suppose that you are trying to reduce your son's screaming every time you tell him to go to bed. It wouldn't make much sense for you to keep track of his yelling during breakfast. Collect data only when you think the behavior is most problematic. However, if you do not know when the behavior is likely to occur, or if it seems as though it is a constant phenomenon, then record data at various points throughout the day. Maybe this information will help you determine why the behavior is occurring.

Gather Data Over an Extended Period of Time

In addition to gathering data when the behavior is likely to occur, remember to collect data over an extended period of time. This is not to say that you have to record your child's behavior for hours upon end, but rather try to get a sample of the behavior for a few minutes over several days. This is to help ensure that you have an accurate picture of what is going on. After all, if you collect data only once, your information may be skewed. Maybe your child was having an especially good or bad day. Either way, it will be difficult for you to determine what is causing the behavior without accurate information.

STEP 2.5: ANALYZING DATA

Finally, we get to heart of the matter. By now you have identified a target behavior that you want to change. You have collected baseline data on the behavior, taking care to use several different methods. Now you have to look at everything that you have and try to make sense of why your child is doing what she does.

Go back to the first step that we talked about in this chapter (step 2.1) and look at the questions we covered:

- When does the behavior occur?
- Where does the behavior occur?
- Are there people around when the behavior occurs?
- What usually happens before the behavior occurs?
- What happens after the behavior occurs?

Do you see a pattern? Do you have any gut feelings about why your child is acting this way? Take a few minutes to look over all of the information that you have gathered and then write down your conclusions in the following box. You don't have to be certain why the behavior is occurring. But at least try to come up with a working hypothesis or guess. In later chapters we are going to develop an intervention based on your guess and then see if we actually changed the behavior.

_____

_____

_____

APPLYING WHAT YOU HAVE LEARNED

By now, you should have some ideas about how to identify the causes of your child's behaviors (see figure 4.4). This is a crucial step in the behavioral modification process. If you don't know what causes the behavior, it becomes almost impossible to effectively change it.

Let's apply what you have learned in this chapter. Go back and reread the case study at the beginning of the chapter. Then answer the questions following the case study.

Question 1: Why Is It Important to Know When Ahib Is Acting Inappropriately and When He Is Not?

Imagine that Ahib is your child. He is normally very well behaved, but suddenly a couple of teachers start complaining that he is talking too much in class. One of the first things that you would want to determine is when he is acting inappropriately and when he is behaving himself. Why is this so important?

There are many potential explanations for why Ahib is talking when he shouldn't. Perhaps he is bored in class because it is too easy or too hard. Maybe he can't hear what the teacher is saying so he is asking the people around him what is going on. Or maybe, as Ms. Salizar surmised, he likes the girl sitting next to him.

Determining when the behavior occurs and when it does not is often very useful in figuring out why the behavior is occurring. Clearly, if Ahib is only talking in one or two environments, and not others, those environments probably hold the key to understanding the behavior. Further, by looking at when he is not talking, we can get valuable insights as to what strategies might help him behave more appropriately.

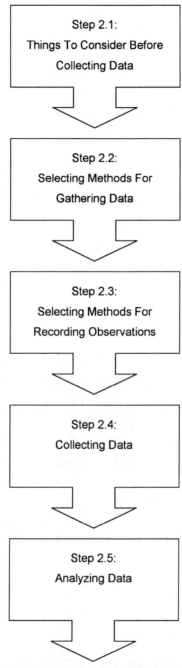

Figure 4.4   Flow Chart of Step 2.

Question 2: How Could Ms. Salizar Either Confirm or Refute Her Hypothesis Regarding the Cause of Ahib's Behavior?

When attempting to figure out what is causing your child's behavior, you should gather data in as many ways as possible. This will help you collect a broad array of information. The more information you gather, the clearer the picture you will have and the stronger your hypothesis will be.

After thinking about her son's behavior, Ms. Salizar concluded that he was talking in class because he liked the girl who sat next to him. However, at this point, this is just an educated guess. How could Ms. Salizar either confirm or refute her hypothesis?

Perhaps the easiest way to confirm or refute her hypothesis is to see if Ahib talks as much when the girl is there compared to when she is not there. Ahib's teachers can simply keep track of Ahib's behavior when the girl is present and compare it to when she is absent. They could also move Ahib's seat away from the girl to see if this has any effect on his behavior. If it decreases his talking, Ms. Salizar's conclusion would appear to be correct.

Question 3: If Somebody Were to Observe Ahib in the Two Classes, What Recording Schedules Should Probably Be Used?

Observation is a key method to collect data on behavior. It is a flexible way of considering many factors all at once. Recording data from observations could be done in many ways. However, each way has its strengths and weaknesses. What recording schedule should be used to measure Ahib's behavior?

When selecting a recording schedule, the first thing you should consider is the behavior that you are measuring. Ahib's behavior involves talking, which does not lend itself to an actual frequency count. After all, how would you measure one "unit of talking?" For instance, do you measure each word spoken? Do you count each new conversation? How do you define "conversation?"

Further, when considering a data collection schedule, you must think about what kind of data you want. For instance, if you want the length of time that Ahib talks, you could use duration recording. On the other hand, if you want to get a picture of how often Ahib is talking, then you could use time sampling or interval recording.

5

STEP 3: DEVELOPING AN INTERVENTION: INCREASING APPROPRIATE BEHAVIOR

CHAPTER OBJECTIVES

By the time you complete this chapter, you should be able to:

- Define reinforcement.
- Identify different types of reinforcement.
- Give examples of positive, negative, natural, artificial, primary, and secondary reinforcers.
- Identify possible reinforcers that could help increase your child's appropriate behaviors.
- Determine when to use reinforcers with your child.

CASE STUDY OF CHRISSY AND ANN WORINSKI

Siblings are known to fight on occasion. It is just natural that when you live with somebody for so long, you will have a quarrel every now and again. However, when Chrissy and Ann get together, the fur really flies. In fact, in one of their last scraps, Chrissy gave Ann a black eye and Chrissy got a cut on her head that required seven stitches.

Chrissy and Ann's father has tried many things in an effort to stop the fighting. He tried spanking them. He tried sending them both to time out. He has taken away their toys. He has begged and pleaded. He has ordered and threatened. But nothing seems to stop them from going at it. Eventually their father sat down at the kitchen table and tried to come up with something new.

He realized that everything that he had tried involved stopping the fighting by using punishment. This obviously wasn't working. But what else could he do? Then the idea came to him. He could try encouraging them to play nicely together. Perhaps he could find some sort of reward that would make playing nicely together worth it. But what would be something that they both liked that was so important to them that they would stop fighting to get it?

He walked around the house to get some ideas. They liked to play video games. There was a stack of them by the television set. Perhaps he could get them a video game if they played nicely. The problem with that was, he realized, his daughters would probably fight over the video games. Plus he couldn't afford to get them a new game every time they were nice.

He continued looking around. In their bedrooms were lots of stuffed animals. He could reward them with stuffed animals, but again, he would have to buy too many of them if the behavior actually caught on.

He needed something small and inexpensive. It also had to be something that they liked enough so that they would want to earn it. He kept looking around, but nothing occurred to him. In the end he just decided to give them candy every time they played well together. "After all," he thought, "all kids like candy."

CASE STUDY QUESTIONS

Question 1: What kind of reinforcement and schedule did Mr. Worinski end up using?

Question 2: What problems could Mr. Worinski experience when trying to implement his reward program?

Question 3: What other types of reinforcement and schedules could he have used?

INTRODUCTION

You should have some clue as to why the target behavior you selected in chapter 3 is happening. You should also have data that show how frequent or severe the behavior is before you intervene. Now we are going to develop an intervention plan.

Intervention plans outline how you are going to attempt to change the behavior. Typically they involve some sort of reinforcement and punishment. In this chapter we discuss reinforcing behavior. In chapter 6 we take a look at punishing behavior.

DEFINING REINFORCEMENT

What do you think of when you hear the words "reward" or "reinforcement?" Maybe you think of a wanted poster from the old West promising money for the capture of notorious criminals. Or maybe you think of a teacher giving students an extra five minutes of recess if they do well on a spelling test. Both of these can be considered examples of reinforcement. They can also be examples of punishment. Confused? Let's get everything straightened out.

Reinforcement is the process by which the target behavior is increased or strengthened (e.g., increasing its duration or magnitude). As we will discuss later, this process can be internal, such as when you feel good about doing something, or external, such as when somebody gives you something for performing a certain action.

As with punishment, reinforcement should be used with great caution. Overuse could devalue the reinforcer and make it worthless in the eyes of your child. It could also make your child's behavior dependent on getting something in return. Further, reinforcers can actually become punishers, as we will discuss shortly. Consequently, it is important that you understand what reinforcement is and how to use it appropriately.

TYPES OF REINFORCEMENT

Think about the different ways that you can increase your child's appropriate behavior. You are probably coming up with different types of reinforcers, although maybe you don't know it. There are several categories of reinforcers, including:

- Positive reinforcement
- Negative reinforcement
- Natural reinforcers
- Artificial reinforcers
- Primary reinforcers
- Secondary reinforcers

Positive Reinforcement

Positive reinforcement involves increasing the desired behavior by giving the child something that he or she likes. Sounds simple, doesn't it? It really isn't. Consider the following examples:

1. A student gets $10 for every "A" on her report card.
2. A student gets sent to "time out" if she talks in class.
3. A parent smiles and says "good job" whenever the child does something correctly.
4. The child can watch television for an hour if she cleans her room.
5. The child does not have to do his chores if he doesn't throw a temper tantrum all week.

Which of these are examples of positive reinforcement? The answer is, "it depends." You see, what is considered a reinforcer depends on the child's perspective. If the child does not want $10, praise from a parent, or an hour of television, these outcomes would not increase the desired behavior. Remember that what may be desirable for one person may not be seen as desirable by another. For example, do you like broccoli? Some people do and some don't. The point is, if your parents offered you broccoli every time you did something they wanted, you might or might not be encouraged to perform the behavior in question.

Look at example 2, giving a student a "time out." You may have said that this was a punishment, not a reward. But again, it depends on the perspective of the child. Imagine that you were in a class that you just hated. You had no idea what was going on. Your teacher made you feel stupid and your classmates made fun of you. Would being sent to the time out room increase or decrease your talking behavior? It probably would actually increase your talking. So, in essence, being sent to time out could actually be a reinforcer, even though the teacher thinks it is a punishment. This is an extremely important concept to keep in mind when developing a behavioral modification program for your children.

So think about your child and the behavior that you want to increase. In the space below, brainstorm a list of ways that you could use positive reinforcement to help your child. You don't have to develop anything fancy. In fact, you may later decide that you don't want to use positive reinforcement. The idea is for you to generate some potential ways to improve your child's behavior by giving him something that he likes if he performs the desired behavior.

_____

_____

_____

Negative Reinforcement

Whereas positive reinforcement increases appropriate behavior by giving something to the child that she wants, negative reinforcement increases appropriate behavior by taking something away that she doesn't want. This might sound like punishment, but as we will discuss in this and the following chapters, there is a very subtle and significant different. Perhaps a few examples might help. Which of the following would be considered negative reinforcement?

1. Every time your child eats all of his dinner, he gets to use the computer for an hour.
2. If your child gets a perfect score on her spelling pre-test, she doesn't have to take the post-test.
3. If your child finishes his homework, he gets dessert with his dinner.
4. Every time your child gets into a fight, you take away 10 good behavior points.
5. If your child gets a good report card, you take away his curfew.

Remember, reinforcement increases appropriate behavior. Negative reinforcement increases appropriate behavior by taking away something that the child doesn't like. Which of the above meet that criterion? Hopefully you are thinking, "Well, it depends on whether the child likes or doesn't like all of those things." That is exactly right! But let's assume that your child doesn't like using the computer, taking post-tests, eating dessert, getting points taken away, and having a curfew. Which of the above could then be considered negative reinforcement?

In scenario 1, the child is getting something that he doesn't like for eating all of his dinner. Would his appropriate behavior (i.e., eating his dinner) increase or decrease? It would probably decrease. After all, you are actually punishing him for eating his dinner since he doesn't like using the computer. So this would not be negative reinforcement.

How about the second scenario? Here, if the child gets a perfect score on the spelling pre-test, she doesn't have to take the post-test. Remember, she doesn't like taking the post-test. So will her appropriate behavior (e.g., doing well on the pre-test) likely increase or decrease? Hopefully, it will increase. So, is this an example of positive or negative reinforcement? Since you are rewarding good behavior by taking away something that she doesn't like, this would be an example of negative reinforcement. The same is true for scenario 5.

Again, take a few minutes to think about the specific situation that you and your child are facing. How could you use negative reinforcement to encourage your child to perform the desired behavior? Use the lines below to brainstorm a list of ideas. Again, you want to think of things that your child does not like that you can take away if he performs the desired behavior.

_____

_____

_____

Natural and Artificial Reinforcers

In addition to using positive or negative reinforcement, you can also use natural or artificial reinforcers. Natural reinforcers are those that occur as an ordinary outcome from the appropriate behavior. For example, if you clean your room and feel good about it, that feeling is a natural reinforcer. Artificial reinforcers are those that are created by a parent or teacher specifically to modify the child's behavior.

For instance, suppose that you implemented a reward system whereby if your child goes to bed on time without an argument, he gets a check by his name on the refrigerator. If he gets three checks in a row, he will be allowed to go get pizza (which he likes). In this example, you are using positive reinforcement (e.g., your child is increasing behavior to get something that he likes) and artificial reinforcers (e.g., the checks that you give for appropriate behavior). Make sense?

Ideally all reinforcers would be natural reinforcers. After all, you don't want your child to be nice to other people because he is getting a pizza party at the end of the month. You want him to behave appropriately because it is the right thing to do. So eventually it is wise to gradually fade artificial reinforcers so that your child's behavior doesn't become dependent on them.

Primary and Secondary Reinforcers

In addition to being natural or artificial, the outcomes that you use to increase the desired behavior can also be primary or secondary reinforcers. Both can be effective in promoting appropriate behavior. However, they each have different strengths and weaknesses.

Primary reinforcers are those that are innately motivating. That is, you do not have to teach a child to like the reinforcer. They include things that we need to continue living, such as food, water, and sleep. You do not have to teach a child to want food or something to drink. It is a biological necessity.

Whereas primary reinforcers are naturally motivating, secondary reinforcers must be learned. For example, if your child does what you ask and you give her a sticker with a big smiley face on it, she probably would not be rewarded naturally. After all, stickers have no intrinsic value to children. They have to be taught that such things are desirable.

Primary reinforcers are often used to produce a quick result. So if you need to get your child to do something right away, primary reinforcers are probably your best bet. Primary reinforcers are also best when working with young children or children with mental retardation because

they may not understand the value associated with secondary reinforcers.

However, you cannot always use food and other primary reinforcers
to get what you want. Think about it. What if you were given a piece of
candy every time you did what somebody wanted? After a while, you
probably would get sick of the candy or would no longer be hungry. As
a result, it would not be a reinforcer anymore. Further, too much candy
could be harmful. This is why it is often beneficial to use secondary reinforcers.

So can you tell the difference between primary and secondary reinforcers? Let's see. Look at the potential reinforcers listed below. Which
do you think are primary reinforcers? Which do you think are secondary reinforcers? For simplicity's sake, assume that your child likes each
of these:

1. Social interactions
2. Being given money
3. Smiles
4. Being excused from doing homework
5. Being given more play time

So which of these can be considered primary reinforcers and which
are secondary reinforcers? There is a little wiggle room here, but basically options 2 and 4 are definitely secondary. After all, money doesn't
naturally have any value. You have to be taught that you can trade in
money for things that you want. Further, despite what some students
might think, homework is not intrinsically good or bad. Students learn
to react to homework positively or negatively after experiencing it.

Options 1, 3, and 5 can be argued either way. However, a great deal
of research has indicated that humans are social animals and that, without social interactions, we get sick easier and die younger. Consequently,
you could say that social interactions are primary reinforcers.

But what about smiling? Smiling seems to be universal. Every culture
in the world smiles. In fact, very young infants respond positively to the
smiles of their parents. So you could also correctly believe that getting a
smile from somebody is innately reinforcing and therefore a primary reinforcer.

Finally, we need to exercise to keep in good health. You can also support the assertion that we need recreational activities to handle unhealthy stress. But is being allowed to play more a natural reinforcer? Or do you have to be taught that playing is good? These are questions for the ages.

STEP 3.1: BRAINSTORMING POSSIBLE REINFORCERS FOR YOUR CHILD

Hopefully by now you understand a bit more about reinforcers. As we discussed at the beginning of this chapter, it is probably a more complicated topic than you thought. After all, what is a reinforcer often depends on the perspective of the child, not what you think should be rewarding. So how do you know what is rewarding for your child? Great question!

The first step in finding a good reinforcer is to know your child. If you know what he or she likes and doesn't like, you are in a good position. How can you find out what your child likes? Following are some steps that you can take to find out.

Ask Your Child

It sounds simple, but often asking is the most effective way of finding out what your child likes. So take some time over dinner tonight to ask your child what he or she likes and dislikes. Then record the responses in the box below. You might have to ask on several different occasions. After all, the responses that you get might be influenced by the child's mood at the time.

Looking Around the Child's Room

If you have teenagers or children with behavior disorders, asking them what they like probably didn't work. The best response that you got was most likely "I don't know." Further, if you have children with mental retardation, they might not have been able to accurately express their likes and dislikes. So you might want to try some other tactics.

Take a look around your child's room. Don't snoop. Don't dig through his desk drawers or look underneath her mattress, but take a casual look

Likes	Dislikes

Box 5.1   What Your Children Say They Like and Dislike

around. What are on the walls? Are there any posters or pictures? What are they of? What kinds of things are lying around? Are there certain toys or types of toys that your child seems to have? In the lines below, write down your observations.

_____

_____

_____

Observe Your Child

Another good way of figuring out what your child thinks is rein-forcing is to observe her. You don't have to spy or hire a private investigator, merely watch what she does and listen to what she says. What does she talk to her friends about? What kinds of television and computer programs does she like? Does she like to read? What kinds of books does she like? What does she do on a rainy day? What does she do with her friends? Does she play any sports or games? What kinds of food does she like to eat? In the lines below, record your observations.

_____

_____

_____

Other Thoughts

You can get ideas for reinforcers from many places. For example, are there any academic subjects that your child is particularly good at? What does he draw in the margins of his school notebooks? Do his teachers or friends have any ideas for effective reinforcers? Indicate these ideas in the lines below.

_____

_____

_____

STEP 3.2: IDENTIFYING REINFORCERS FOR YOUR CHILD

Take a few minutes to review the lists that you made as a result of talking to your child, looking around his bedroom, and observing him in multiple environments. You should have a long list of potential reinforcers that you could use to modify your child's behavior. Use the following space to list some of your more promising possibilities.

_____

_____

_____

Now you need to narrow this long list down to a select few that you feel will work the best. How do you know which possibilities are the best to use? Consider these important variables:

- Manipulability
- Palatability
- Accessibility

After reading the following sections, look through your lists of potential reinforcers and identify the ones that might work best for your child. Write these in the space that follows the section on accessibility.

Manipulability

The first thing you should ask yourself when trying to find a good reinforcer is, "Can I manipulate it?" That is, can you give it and take it away easily? For example, suppose that your child likes using the computer. Time on the computer is something that you can easily give and take away. This might make a good reinforcer.

Suppose that your child likes to play baseball. In fact, he plays on a little league team. You could use this as a reinforcer. For example, you might tell him that he can't play this week if he doesn't clean his room. However, think about how this might affect the rest of his team. They are probably counting on him to play. Further, his lack of playing one week might affect his ability to play the following weeks.

Food might be a good reinforcer, too. But can you take it away? Not really. Or at least, not for very long.

The trick is to find a reinforcer that you can use without too much hassle, but that will also encourage your child to do what you ask. It also helps if the reinforcer has increments, such as number of hours on the computer or number of innings played. That way you can dole out the reinforcer bit by bit, rather than in large chunks, so that the amount of reinforcer can be modified to match the value of your child's behavior.

Palatability

Good reinforcers have to have staying power. That is, the influence that they have over your child has to last. Look through your list of possible reinforcers. Are there any that your child would get sick of fairly quickly? You don't want to use reinforcers that are not going to be rewarding after your child has obtained them once or twice. So make sure you select something that the child will like after repeated exposure to it.

Then again, there is nothing that says you can't use multiple reinforcers. For example, maybe you have a list of five different things that your child likes (e.g., pizza, playing cards, staying up late, having a sleepover with friends, etc.). You could use all five of these reinforcers intermittently. You could even allow your child to choose what she wants as a reward!

Accessibility

Let's suppose that you found something that your child really likes, such as chocolate. She will do anything to get this reward. So when you offer it to her, she is very willing to increase the desired behavior. Unfortunately, she realizes that she doesn't need you to get the reward. She could go to the local candy shop and buy her own chocolate! Would she still try to earn the reinforcer?

If a reward is too accessible, it is difficult to manipulate it. An effective reward has to be rare enough that the child has to perform the desired behavior to get it. This is basic economics. After all, if gold could be found in everybody's back yard, it probably would not be worth much.

_____

_____

_____

STEP 3.3: DETERMINING WHEN TO USE REINFORCERS

The key to using reinforcement successfully is not only to use things that are actually reinforcing from your child's perspective but also to ensure that you use the reinforcers at the appropriate times. But before you can determine when to use reinforcement, you will need to understand the options available to you. There are several schedules for rewarding behaviors (see table 5.1), including:

Table 5.1   Summary of Reinforcement Schedules

Reinforcement Schedule	Summary
Constant	The behavior is reinforced each and every time it occurs
Fixed-Ratio	The behavior is reinforced each set amount of times that it occurs (e.g., every five times)
Fixed-Interval	The behavior is reinforced each set amount of times that the behavior lasts (e.g., after every ten minutes)
Variable-Ratio	The behavior is reinforced roughly every so many times
Variable-Interval	The behavior is reinforced roughly every so much amount of time it lasts

- Constant
- Fixed-ratio
- Fixed-interval
- Variable-ratio
- Variable-interval

Constant

Let's suppose that your parents wanted to increase the likelihood that you will say nice things to your brother. Since they want to increase appropriate behavior, they use a reinforcement—giving you a piece of candy. If they gave you a piece of candy each time you said something nice to your brother, they would be using a constant schedule for (positively) reinforcing your behavior. That is, each time the target behavior occurs, the person gets rewarded.

Strengths.   The principal strength of constant reinforcement is that students realize very quickly that the target behavior is associated with the positive outcome. Consequently, your child is more likely to acquire the behavior than if you use other methods. Because of this, constant reinforcement is often used when the target behavior is extremely important for the child to learn right away, such as when safety is an issue (e.g., looking both ways before crossing the street). Constant reinforcement is also useful when children may not understand that they are being reinforced for a specific behavior, such as when they are very young or have mental retardation.

Weaknesses.   There are two primary weaknesses of constantly reinforcing behavior. The first is that reinforcers typically lose their power when they are overused. Think about the example that we discussed above. Suppose that every time you said something nice to your brother, your parents gave you a piece of candy. After a few nice comments, you would probably start getting full and might no longer want any more candy. In other words, the candy ceases to be a reinforcer.

To further illustrate how reinforcers can weaken over time, imagine that somebody always compliments you on how you look. That person says, "Oh, you look great!" every day, even if you are wearing the ugliest clothes you own. After a while, you would probably either think that the person was lying or that his fashion standards were pretty low. Either way, his compliments start to lose their value when overused.

The second weakness of constant reinforcement is that the behavior is likely to stop as soon as the reinforcer stops. Imagine that every time you walk down a certain street at a certain time, you find a dollar bill lying on the ground. Needless to say, finding the money is likely to increase your behavior (i.e., walking down that street at that time). However, suppose that after several days of finding money, you walk by the street corner and find nothing. Chances are, you will stop looking for the money soon after you stop finding it. You might think finding the money was just a fluke.

Fixed-Ratio

The second reinforcement schedule that you can use is called "fixed-ratio." To illustrate this approach, let's go back to the example of your parents giving you candy each time you say something nice to your brother. Rather than rewarding you each and every time you say something nice (i.e., a constant schedule), they reward you every set number of times. For example, every third time you say something nice, you get a piece of candy. In other words, you are rewarded on a schedule that occurs after the same number of correct behaviors.

Strengths. One of the strengths of fixed-ratio schedules is that the child's behaviors will not stop right after the reinforcement stops, as is typically the case when constant reinforcement is used. For example, imagine that you found a dollar bill on the street corner every fourth week. For several months, just like clockwork, you find a dollar right where you expected to find it, so you keep walking by that corner. However, one week it is not there when it should be. So you probably think to yourself, "Hmm. That is strange. Let's see if it is there next time." So you keep going by the street corner and find that it is not there four weeks later. In other words, you had to complete the entire rotation to see if the reward was going to be there the next time.

Weaknesses.   When a child has to wait to be reinforced, he or she is less likely to understand that there is a connection between the behavior and the positive outcome. As a result, the child might not perform the desired behavior. Further, performance during the non-reward times tends to be weak. Think about it this way. Let's suppose that your teachers praised you every third time you tried to answer a question in class. You would probably rush the first two attempts to get to the third and be rewarded quicker. The first two attempts might be wrong because they were rushed.

Fixed-Interval

Whereas fixed-ratio rewards children after a set number of correct behaviors, fixed-interval rewards children after a set amount of time. For example, if you were trying to increase the length of time your child studied, you might reward her for every five minutes that she practiced her math facts.

Strengths.   Fixed-interval schedules are very useful for getting somebody started on a routine. Fixed intervals are wonderful at producing quick changes in behavior. However, the reward interval can't be too far apart, or it will not be reinforcing.

Weaknesses.   One downside to fixed-interval schedules is that they can only be used for behaviors where time is a factor. For example, if your parents were trying to increase the number of times that you complimented your brother, fixed-interval wouldn't work. Whenever you want to increase the number of times something happens, you probably want to use a ratio schedule. However, fixed-interval could be perfect if your parents wanted to increase the amount of time that you played with your brother.

Second, children can learn to expect that they are going to be reinforced after a certain time. So the thought of being rewarded might actually stop them from doing what you want them to do. For instance, suppose that you were going to praise your daughter every five minutes that she studies. It would be pretty difficult for her to keep her attention on studying if you kept patting her on the back and saying "Good job!"

Variable-Ratio

With fixed-ratio, you would reward your child consistently after the same number of appropriate behaviors, such as every fourth time he completes a task. With variable-ratio, you would reward your child roughly after the same number of times the appropriate behavior was performed, but not exactly. For instance, if you used variable-ratio, you might reinforce the second time the appropriate behavior occurred, then the sixth time, then the fifth, then the third—so the average reinforcement time would be four.

Strengths.   One of the primary strengths of variable-ratio schedules is that your child will not know exactly when she will be reinforced. As a result, your child will probably continue the desired behavior longer than if a fixed-ratio schedule were used. If you think about it from the child's perspective, this would make sense. If your child gets rewarded roughly every five times, she will never really know if this is the time she will get reinforced. So if she doesn't get reinforced for a few behaviors, she will probably think, "Oh, I bet I will get something next time." So she will perform the behavior again. Then if she doesn't get reinforced that time either, she probably would think, "Boy! I will definitely get reinforced the next time." So she will perform the behavior again, and so on, and so on.

Weaknesses.   One of the potential weaknesses of variable-ratio is that it could confuse your child. He might refuse to continue performing the behavior because he thinks that you forgot to reward him. Further, if your child does not know when the reinforcer is coming, he might look for it after each behavior. Consequently, this constant anticipation of the reinforcer could distract him from the task at hand.

Variable-Interval

So what do you think a variable-interval schedule would be? Basically, it is the same as a variable-ratio schedule, but the behavior is rewarded after time has passed rather than after an average number of specific behaviors. So you might reinforce a behavior after it has occurred for three minutes, then after seven minutes, and then after nine minutes, and then after one minute. The average interval that would be reinforced would be every five minutes.

Strengths. As with variable-ratio, variable-interval schedules promote the desired behavior well after reinforcement has stopped. As described previously, your child will never really know when she will be reinforced. So she will keep performing the behavior hoping that if she does so for a little longer, she will be rewarded.

Weaknesses. Also as with variable-ratio, variable-interval schedules might confuse your child. He may stop the behavior because he thought that he deserved a reward and didn't get it. Further, variable schedules are less likely to promote new behaviors compared to constant or fixed schedules.

STEP 3.4: DETERMINING WHAT TYPE OF REINFORCERS TO USE

Now that you have a general idea about reinforcement schedules, you are probably thinking, "Well, which one do I use?" In the end, you will be the one who has to decide, but here are some questions that might be of help:

- How urgent is the change?
- How motivated will your child be to earn the reward?
- Are you trying to increase the time or frequency of the behavior?
- Will your child have difficulty understanding that there is a link between the behavior and the reward?

If you need to change the behavior right away, consider using a constant reinforcement schedule. You could also use a fixed-ratio reinforcement schedule in which the behavior is reinforced very frequently. Both of these schedules will also help if your child has difficulty understanding the link between the behavior and the outcome.

If your child is willing to work for the reward, you can try spreading out the reinforcers. Fixed and variable schedules are good ways of doing this. However, take care not to spread the reinforcers out so far apart that your child is no longer motivated to earn them.

If you are trying to change a behavior that involves time, such as the length of time studying or sitting still, use an interval schedule. If you are changing a behavior that involves frequency, such as trying to increase the amount of homework completed or number of positive comments that your child makes, then ratio schedules are your best bet.

STEP 3.5: BRAINSTORMING WAYS OF INCREASING APPROPRIATE BEHAVIOR

By now, you should have a good idea about different ways of increasing your child's appropriate behavior. Now you need to sit down and think of all the different things that you could do to encourage your child to do what you want her to do. In the box below, brainstorm ideas for each method of increasing behavior. You might want to review what you wrote earlier in the chapter. Remember, you aren't trying to develop the final idea just yet. So write down anything that comes to mind. We will fine tune it later.

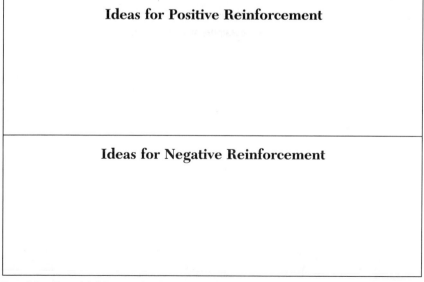

Ideas for Positive Reinforcement

Ideas for Negative Reinforcement

Box 5.2   Potential Strategies for Increasing Your Child's Appropriate Behavior

Box 5.2   (Continued)

Ideas for Natural Reinforcers
Ideas for Artificial Reinforcers
Ideas for Primary Reinforcers
Ideas for Secondary Reinforcers

STEP 3.6: DEVELOPING A REINFORCEMENT PLAN

In the last section, you brainstormed ideas that could encourage your child to increase his appropriate behavior. Now we need to develop a formalized plan. Here are some activities that might help.

Prioritizing Strategies

You are probably having a difficult time narrowing down the potential ways that you could reinforce your child's appropriate behavior. So you will probably have to prioritize some of your ideas. But how do you do that?

Natural and primary reinforcers first. The end result of behavior modification programs should be to replace inappropriate behavior with appropriate behavior. Further, the program should not be continued indefinitely. After all, someday your child will be living on her own and she will not have somebody offering her a cookie every time she picks up her clothes or plays nicely with others. Consequently, you might want to consider using reinforcers that are natural and primary first. This will save you time trying to wean your child off the artificial and secondary reinforcers.

Go back and look at the ideas for reinforcers that you brainstormed in the last box. In the following lines, write down those ideas that involve reinforcers that are natural and primary.

_____

_____

_____

If you could not think of any natural or primary reinforcers, list the reinforcers that are the least contrived. That is, list the ones that would seem the closest to being natural. For example, paying your child with real money to clean her room is more natural than an elaborate token economy with plastic poker chips as rewards.

Most effective. In the lines above, you probably have many ideas from which to choose. So you may have to prioritize them even further. Go back and look at what you have written. Now, in the following space write down the top five or six ideas that you think will be the most effective in changing your child's behavior.

_____

_____

_____

Easiest. Depending on how many ideas you brainstormed earlier, you might still have several potential strategies for increasing your child's appropriate behaviors. So how do you choose from those that remain? If all else is equal about the strategies, that is, they are all likely to be effective, you might want to select the strategy that is easiest to implement. In the lines below, list the strategies that you have written in the box immediately above in the order of easiest to hardest.

_____

_____

_____

Final Plan

By this point, you should have come up with a short list of potential strategies that can encourage your child to increase his appropriate behavior. Now you will need to select one that you will actually use. You might want to pick one of the top two or three listed in the last box; however, in the end, you might want to go with whatever your intuition tells you. Simply ask yourself, "What do I think will work best?" Then write that strategy down in the following lines and include the type of reinforcement schedule that you want to use (see step 3.3).

_____

_____

_____

Backup Plan

Thought you were done? Not yet. Frequently your first attempt at changing behavior will not work. In such cases you will need a fall-back plan. In the lines below, write down a second strategy for increasing your child's desired behavior. This will be your backup plan in case your final plan doesn't work as well as you want. Don't forget to include the reinforcement schedule that you want to use.

_____

_____

_____

APPLYING WHAT YOU HAVE LEARNED

As we discussed throughout this chapter, using reinforcement is often a tricky business (see figure 5.1). It certainly isn't as easy as most people think. Not only are there different types of reinforcers, but how often you use them will have a profound effect on your ability to change your child's behavior. Moreover, what is reinforcing to one person is not always reinforcing to another. In fact, what is once considered a reinforcer could quickly be seen as a punisher, as we will discuss in the next chapter.

Take a few minutes to re-read the case study at the beginning of the chapter. Think about the questions that appear after it. Next we will apply what you have learned in the chapter to the case study.

Question 1: What Kind of Reinforcement and Schedule Did Mr. Worinski End Up Using?

Mr. Worinski could have used a number of different types of reinforcers and schedules. For example, he could have used negative reinforcement or artificial reinforcers on a variable-ratio schedule. What kind of reinforcement and schedule did he end up using?

Since Mr. Worinski was giving his daughters something that they (supposedly) liked to increase their appropriate behavior, he was using positive reinforcement. He was also using a natural reinforcer (i.e., candy/food). The candy also can be considered a primary reinforcer, if in fact the girls liked the kind of candy they were given and they were hungry.

What about the schedule of reinforcement? What kind of schedule did Mr. Worinski use? Because he gave them a reward each and every time they performed the desire behavior, he was using a constant schedule.

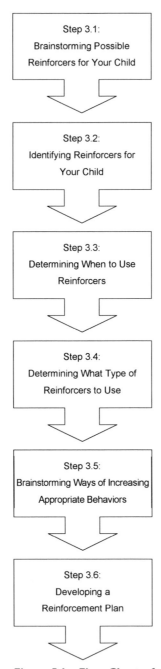

Figure 5.1 Flow Chart of Step 3

Question 2: What Problems Could Mr. Worinski Experience When Trying to Implement His Reward Program?

As mentioned previously, using reinforcement isn't as easy as many people think. From the sound of it, Mr. Worinski seemed to believe that he would simply offer candy to his daughters every time they played well together. However, there are many things that could go awry. What are some of the problems that Mr. Worinski might experience when implementing his reward program?

It would take a long time to list all the difficulties that Mr. Worinski might face; however, there are some very obvious and likely problems. For instance, one of the weaknesses of using a constant reinforcement schedule is that the reinforcer could lose its power pretty quickly. So in other words, after getting a few pieces of candy his daughters may not want the reinforcement any more.

Further, the problem with using candy as a reinforcer is that children can usually get their own candy. So it may not have much appeal to them even if they like candy to begin with. After all, why would they want to be nice to each other if they could simply buy their own reward?

Question 3: What Other Types of Reinforcement and Schedules Could He Have Used?

There are many different reinforcement programs that can be developed. However, you have to be able to choose the right type of reinforcement and schedule to suit your needs. Other than what Mr. Worinski came up with, what other types of reinforcement systems and schedules could he have used?

Rather than using a positive reinforcement system (i.e., giving them something they like when the appropriate behavior occurs), Mr. Worinski could have used negative reinforcement. For instance, he could have taken away something that his daughters didn't like, such as their weekly chores, if they got along. He also could have used an artificial reinforcer, such as money, or tried to get them to feel good about interacting appropriately, which is a primary reinforcer.

6

STEP 4: DEVELOPING AN INTERVENTION: DECREASING INAPPROPRIATE BEHAVIOR

CHAPTER OBJECTIVES

By the time you complete this chapter, you should be able to:

- Define punishment.
- List ways of decreasing inappropriate behaviors.
- Explain the strengths and weaknesses of each way to decrease inappropriate behaviors.
- Identify strategies to decrease your child's target behavior.
- Consider ethical dilemmas associated with using punishments.

CASE STUDY OF GREGORY MUNOZ

Gregory Munoz is a young child with autism and mental retardation. His parents and teachers are very concerned about his behavior and do not know what to do. Specifically, Gregory self-abuses at an extremely high rate. He will bang his forehead on the ground and walls and hit himself in the temple with his fist or anything that he can get his hands on. Moreover, his behavior is so severe he is at risk of causing permanent brain damage.

The Munozes and Gregory's special education teachers have studied the behavior and believe that it is triggered whenever Gregory is upset. They have developed a long list of things that are likely to set Gregory off, including environmental changes, being touched, and sudden noises. For his own protection, Gregory wears a bicycle helmet. Unfortunately, wearing this helmet is one of the triggers for his behavior. So when wearing it, he will go into an uncontrollable rage, hitting and biting himself as well as others, until he is too exhausted to move. Both the Munozes and Gregory's teachers feel that the helmet is simply a stopgap measure and that they need to somehow stop Gregory from self-abusing.

Thus far, many different types of reinforcement plans have been tried. But they have not been successful. Several of the special educators feel that an intervention needs to be developed that combines rewarding Gregory for not self-abusing and punishing him when he does.

CASE STUDY QUESTIONS

Question 1: When developing a behavioral modification program, what problems might arise because Gregory has mental retardation?

Question 2: What behavior-reducing strategies might be appropriate for Gregory?

Question 3: What behavior-reducing strategies would not be appropriate for Gregory?

INTRODUCTION

Throughout the last chapter, we discussed how to increase your child's appropriate behavior. As you know, this can be done by using various forms of reinforcement. This chapter focuses on how to decrease inappropriate behavior. As you will learn, this can be done by using punishment.

What do you think of when you hear the word "punishment?" For many people, the term "punishment" has many negative connotations. They think of prisons, electrical shocks, and various forms of medieval tortures. In fact, you might be thinking to yourself, "I really don't want to punish my kid. I don't believe in spanking."

Spanking can certainly be considered a punishment. However, as we discuss in greater detail in this chapter, there are many ways of reducing inappropriate behaviors that do not involve striking your child. Perhaps you will find one that suits your needs.

The concept of punishment is often misunderstood; it is not as horrible as it sounds. In fact, most effective behavioral modification programs include some sort of punishment to help reduce inappropriate behavior as well as some sort of reinforcement component to increase appropriate behavior. In this chapter we discuss what punishment is, how to use it effectively, as well as many other ways of decreasing inappropriate behaviors.

METHODS OF REDUCING INAPPROPRIATE BEHAVIOR

Before we can go on and start developing methods for you to reduce your child's inappropriate behaviors, we first must discuss your options. There are many different strategies for diminishing the frequency or intensity of behavior. Each has strengths and weaknesses (see table 6.1). It is important for you to know the difference as well as to select the strategy that meets your needs. In this section, we discuss several methods for reducing behavior, including:

- Promoting incompatible behaviors
- Promoting more appropriate behaviors
- Promoting a reduction of the inappropriate behavior
- Response-cost
- Presenting aversive stimuli for inappropriate behavior
- Making the inappropriate behavior nonreinforcing

Promoting Incompatible Behaviors

Hold this book with both hands. Now try to throw a pencil across the room. It is difficult to do when you don't have a free hand, isn't it? One way to reduce inappropriate behaviors is to have your child perform

Table 6.1   Summary of Methods for Reducing Inappropriate Behavior

Method	Summary
Promoting Incompatible Behaviors	Having your child perform an action that prevents him from performing the target behavior at the same time
Promoting More Appropriate Behaviors	Teaching your child a more acceptable way of getting what the target behavior accomplishes
Promoting a Reduction of the Inappropriate Behavior	Rewarding your child if the target behavior decreases
Response-Cost	Taking away something that your child likes if the target behavior occurs
Presenting Aversive Stimuli for Inappropriate Behavior	Giving something that your child doesn't like if the target behavior occurs
Making the Inappropriate Behavior Nonreinforcing	Breaking the association that makes the target behavior fun to perform

other behaviors that prevent the inappropriate behaviors from occurring. In other words, if your hands are already full, it is difficult to pick up a pencil and throw it across the room.

This strategy is often very effective when the replacement behavior is more valued by the child than is the inappropriate behavior. Further, you should choose a replacement behavior that is actually beneficial to learn. Otherwise you might have to replace the new behavior later on.

Now think about the target behavior that you wrote down in chapter 3. Are there any behaviors that could prevent your child from performing the target behavior? In the lines below, try to brainstorm a list of prevention behaviors that you could use to decrease the likelihood of the target behavior occurring.

_____

_____

_____

Now look at the prevention behaviors that you brainstormed. Are any of these prevention behaviors desirable? That is, are any of them something that you would like your child to do? Would your child prefer to perform any of these prevention behaviors more than the target behavior? If so, go back and circle these behaviors. You may have found a very easy way of reducing your child's inappropriate behavior.

Promoting More Appropriate Behaviors

Another way of reducing inappropriate behaviors is to reward other behaviors that are more acceptable and ignore the ones that you don't want. For example, suppose that your child constantly picks on girls in his class. He pushes them. He teases them. He pulls their hair. After going through the process that we described in chapter 4, your hypothesis is that your child is acting this way because he is starting to like girls but doesn't know how to get their attention in an appropriate manner. One way of reducing his poor behavior is to teach him a better way of getting what he wants. So you might teach him how to start a conversation or how to compliment people.

Think again about your child and the target behavior that you are trying to reduce. Are there any behaviors that are more appropriate but still accomplish what your child is trying to do? Consider this for a moment and then, using the lines below, generate a list of potential behaviors that might replace the target behavior.

Promoting a Reduction of the Inappropriate Behavior

Imagine that your child throws violent fits every time you tell her to do something that she doesn't like to do. She will throw things, kick things, scream, and do anything that she can to get her own way. Should you ever reinforce this behavior? Before you say "no," think about it for a moment. What if your child typically throws these fits for 20 minutes, but one day she only carries on for 5 minutes?

By rewarding the gradual reduction of the inappropriate behaviors, you might be able to reduce the frequency or intensity of the behavior to more acceptable levels. However, the trick is to find ways to encourage children to reduce their inappropriate behaviors. To figure out how to do this, look through chapter 5 and identify some outcomes that could be used to reward your child.

Think about the target behavior that you identified previously in this book. What would happen if it was reduced in frequency or intensity? At what frequency or intensity would you be able to tolerate the behavior? These are very important factors that you will need to consider before using this strategy.

Obviously there are some behaviors for which this strategy would not be useful. For instance, if your child was unsafe or potentially harmful to others, you would not want to simply reduce the number of times that he acted inappropriately. After all, running out into the street without looking even once in a while or killing just one person would not be acceptable. However, if a gradual reduction in the target behavior is adequate, maybe this strategy would be a good one for you to try.

Response-Cost

Another strategy for reducing inappropriate behaviors involves taking away things that your child likes every time she performs the inappropriate behavior. For example, if your child does not go to bed when she should, you could take away 10 minutes of television time (assuming that she likes television). This is called response-cost. As the name suggests, whenever the target behavior is performed, the child experiences some sort of cost.

As with any strategy, there are potential pitfalls when using response-cost. For instance, what would happen if your child liked staying up more than she liked watching television? The response-cost strategy probably would not work.

Also, if you are going to use this strategy, make sure that you don't "over-cost" the behavior. For example, imagine that you took away all television time for a week if your child was not in bed exactly at the right time. If your child has already lost everything, why would she care about acting appropriately? After all, she has nothing now to lose by staying up late.

Think about your child and the target behavior that you are trying to decrease. What could you take away each time the behavior occurs? You might want to look at the third through seventh boxes in chapter 5 to remind yourself what your child finds reinforcing. In the following lines, list some of these reinforcers that you could use as part of a response-cost program. You might also want to indicate what should be taken away for every behavior, such as an hour of television or 10 minutes of playtime.

_____

_____

_____

Presenting Aversive Stimuli for Inappropriate Behavior

With response-cost, you would take away something that your child likes every time she does the target behavior. Another strategy is to give your child something that he doesn't like. You might think of this as "classical punishment." For example, maybe your parents spanked you whenever you did something wrong. Assuming that you didn't like to be spanked, this would be an example of presenting an aversive stimulus. Giving your child extra work to do could also be an example of this strategy, if he didn't like homework. However, do not use homework as a punishment. It is difficult enough to get students motivated to learn. By using homework as a punishment, you are basically telling them that learning is a punishment.

What are some of the things that you can use as aversive stimuli? Remember, the stimulus has to be something that your child doesn't like. Further, the punishment must fit the crime, so don't say "Grounding my child for life." Take a few minutes to really think about this. Then jot down what you come up with below.

_____

_____

_____

Making the Inappropriate Behavior Nonreinforcing

A final way to reduce inappropriate behavior is to make the behavior nonreinforcing. As we discussed in chapter 5, behavior that continues over time is usually reinforced somehow. After all, children typically do not willingly do things that they don't want to do. If you make it so that the behavior is not getting reinforced, you can often stop it from occurring.

For example, suppose that a student likes to disrupt class by making noises with his armpit. After collecting data, you guess that the behavior is being reinforced when the other students laugh. If you can prevent the other students from laughing, the behavior will no longer be reinforced, and it should eventually stop. But how could you do this?

One way to prevent the behavior from being reinforced is to use some of the strategies discussed above. For instance, you could take away a minute of recess every time somebody laughs (i.e., response-cost). Or you can give detention to anybody who laughs (i.e., presenting an aversive). Or make your students eat crackers all the time so that they have their mouths full and cannot laugh out loud (i.e., incompatible behaviors). This last option, however, probably would not be very practical.

Another way of preventing the behavior from being reinforced is to make the behavior occur so frequently that it is no longer rewarding. In the above example, you could make the student get up in front of class and make noises for half an hour. After a few minutes the behavior would no longer be funny. The other students would stop laughing and there would be no reason to make the noises anymore.

STEP 4.1: SELECTING METHODS OF DECREASING INAPPROPRIATE BEHAVIOR

At this point, you are probably thinking to yourself, "So what strategy should I use to decrease my child's inappropriate behavior?" This is a good question, and the answer is, "It depends." Following are some general guidelines to help you decide.

Exploring Your Personal Philosophy

Before selecting a strategy to reduce your child's inappropriate behavior, you should examine your personal philosophy and set of ethics. For instance, many people are very opposed to spanking. Others feel that it is a perfectly acceptable way of disciplining their children. Likewise, some people are strongly for or against time outs. In the end, you have to decide what strategies you are comfortable using.

Use the checklist provided in figure 6.1 to help you determine your philosophy. Indicate whether you agree or disagree with the statements. There is also room for you to put any comments that you might have. For example, you might only spank a child if all else has failed. Or you might only use time outs for brief periods of time.

Questions to Consider	Answers and Thoughts
Should an entire group be punished for the actions of one person?	Yes No Maybe **Thoughts:**
Should rewards be taken away once they are earned?	Yes No Maybe **Thoughts:**
Should you use strategies that remove the individual from the environment, such as time out?	Yes No Maybe **Thoughts:**
Should you use punishments that involve physical contact, such as spanking?	Yes No Maybe **Thoughts:**
Should punishments extend over a long period of time (e.g., a week without television) or should they be brief and immediate?	Yes No Maybe **Thoughts:**

Figure 6.1 Questions to Consider When Exploring Your Philosophy about Punishment

STEP 4.2: EXAMINING THE TARGET BEHAVIOR

The next step in determining which method to use to reduce the target behavior is to look at the behavior that you are trying to reduce. As discussed previously, not all strategies are appropriate for all behaviors. Consequently it is very important for you to match the behavior that you are trying to reduce to a strategy that can best achieve your goal.

Perhaps you are thinking, "But how do I know which strategy is correct for the behavior that I want to change?" Here are some quick questions for you to think about. We discuss the implications of each question in the following sections:

- How long has the target behavior been occurring?
- What is the cause of the target behavior?
- Does the frequency or intensity of the target behavior have to go to zero?
- Does the target behavior have to be changed right away?

How Long Has the Target Behavior Been Occurring?

Perhaps the first thing that you should consider when trying to select a method for reducing behavior is to figure out how long the behavior has been occurring. This is important because the longer the behavior has been going on, the harder it will be to change. For instance, if your child has clung to a security blanket for the first six years of her life, giving it up cold turkey might be a bit difficult for her. However, if she has just started to use the security blanket, it would probably be fairly easy for her to give it up.

What Is the Cause of the Target Behavior?

Understanding the cause of the target behavior is a topic to which we keep returning. It is extremely important for you to have some idea why your child is behaving the why he does. For example, if the cause of the behavior is biological in nature, punishments are probably not going to be very effective no matter what strategy you try.

Punishment is only an option if the behavior is the result of willful choice. If your child does not have control over her behavior, then no method of punishment is going to work. If your child cannot control her behavior, you might want to consider accepting the behavior or accommodating it.

If your child does have control over the behavior, you might want to first try to make the behavior nonreinforcing. But to do this you must have a clear idea what is driving the behavior. Maybe if you ignore it or make it occur at even higher frequencies, it will go away.

Does the Frequency or Intensity of the Target Behavior Have to Go to Zero?

Think about the behavior that you are trying to reduce. What would happen if you couldn't eliminate it completely? Would it be okay if the behavior occurred less frequently?

As discussed previously, there are some behaviors that have to be stopped completely. If the behavior fits in this category, then you might want to teach behaviors that make it impossible for your child to conduct the target behavior. When done correctly this strategy could be very effective at completely eliminating inappropriate behaviors. However, if you simply want to reduce the frequency of mildly annoying behavior, then any of the proposed strategies might suit your needs.

Does the Target Behavior Have to Be Changed Right Away?

There are some behaviors that need to be changed right away, such as if your child is self-abusive and in danger of hurting herself. In cases like these, you cannot spend a lot of time trying to wean the child off the behavior. You simply have to stop it right here and now. If this is similar to your situation, you might want to consider presenting an aversive stimulus. Classical punishment is often very effective at changing behavior very quickly. However, as discussed above, you have to be reasonably sure that the behavior is the result of your child's willful choice. If the behavior is not caused by willful choice, you may have to consider behavior-altering medications. But consider this option as your last resort since such medications can have potentially serious side effects.

STEP 4.3: EXAMINING YOUR CHILD

The next step in figuring out how to decrease your child's target behavior is to look at your child. As with the behavior itself, your child may hold many answers as to what strategy would work best for your situation. Consider the following questions:

- Is your child willing to change?
- Does your child understand the connection between behavior and consequences?
- Do you know of good reinforcers to take away?
- Do you know of things that would be effective aversives?

Is Your Child Willing to Change?

If your child is willing to change, you are in very good shape. You probably will not need to do more than develop a program that provides fairly gentle reminders of what is expected. For instance, you might use a response-cost program that takes away something that the child likes every time the target behavior occurs. Or perhaps, instead of inducing a cost, the behavior could result in a warning.

If your child is absolutely against changing her behavior, you will probably have a lot of work to do. You will need to think of ways to "convince" her that changing is going to be in her best interest. That is to say, whatever she gets from performing the behavior is not worth what happens as a result of the behavior (i.e., consequence).

Presenting an aversive stimulus might do the trick. However, so too can teaching the child a behavior that is more appropriate but also gets him what he wants. In the end, if you are able to allow your child to save face by getting something in return for changing his actions, you will come out ahead. The more stubborn the child, the more likely you will have to pair punishment with some rewards.

Does Your Child Understand the Connection Between Behavior and Consequences?

Behavioral modification can become very complicated if you are trying to change the behavior of a child who doesn't understand what is happening. This tends to be the case when the child is very young or has significant mental retardation. In such instances, your child may not understand that if she acts a certain way, then you will take away something that she likes. It may take your child several trials before she begins to catch on, so be patient!

Do You Know of Good Reinforcers to Take Away?

If you know of things that your child values and you are able to take those things away, you could use response-cost strategies. However, the cost must fit the behavior. As mentioned previously, you can't over price the behavior by making the outcome so steep that if the child performs the behavior once he will have nothing to lose by performing it again.

Do You Know of Things That Would Be Effective Aversives?

Presenting an aversive is only effective if your child dislikes the stimulus more than he likes performing the target behavior. Otherwise, the aversive does not have any power. Further, some aversives might actually be reinforcers from the child's perspective. For example, you might not like being yelled at in front of your peers; however, your child might think that it is funny. Or he might think that all of the other kids will see him as being "cool." When developing a strategy, please keep your child's perspective in mind. Otherwise you probably will be wasting your time.

STEP 4.4: BRAINSTORMING WAYS OF REDUCING INAPPROPRIATE BEHAVIORS

Thus far in this chapter we have outlined many different ways of reducing behavior. We have also looked at several important factors that should be considered before selecting a behavior-reducing strategy. Now is the time for you to brainstorm some potential methods to reduce your child's target behavior.

Take some time to digest everything we have covered. Maybe go get a cup of coffee or skim what you have written in the boxes above. Then

think about your child and the target behavior that you are trying to
reduce. In the box below, brainstorm as many potentially useful ideas
for each method as possible. Remember, the key to brainstorming is to
not to overthink. Just write down whatever comes to mind.

Ideas for Promoting Incompatible Behaviors
Ideas for Promoting More Appropriate Behaviors
Ideas for Promoting a Reduction of the Inappropriate Behavior
Ideas for Response-Cost

Box 6.1   Potential Strategies for Reducing Your Child's Target Behavior

Box 6.1   *(Continued)*

<table>
<tr><td colspan="2" align="center">Ideas for Presenting Aversive Stimuli
for Inappropriate Behavior</td></tr>
<tr><td colspan="2" align="center">Ideas for Making the Inappropriate
Behavior Nonreinforcing</td></tr>
</table>

STEP 4.5: DEVELOPING A PLAN

By now you should have a good understanding of how to decrease behavior. You should also have a list of potential strategies for reducing
your child's target behavior. Now you need to formalize a plan. But before you do, following are some considerations to keep in mind.

Prioritizing Strategies

As you look back over the list that you generated in the last box, you
probably came up with several strategies that could do the trick. So you
may be wondering, "Which should I use first?" Good question!

There are two factors to weigh. First, which strategy would be the
easiest to implement? If there is a strategy that is probably going to be
very effective and very easy to use, you might want to use that one first.

However, you should also consider the aversiveness of the strategies
that you want to use. Don't use the most aversive strategy first. After all,
if it doesn't work, what would you do? You need to be able to turn up
the heat if your child still is unwilling to comply with your wishes. Try to
use the least aversive strategy first.

In the box below, prioritize some of the best strategies that you brainstormed during step 4.4. On the left-hand side of the figure, write down the strategies that would be easiest to implement. On the right-hand side of the figure, write down the strategies in order of their aggressiveness (from least aversive to most).

Easiest Strategies	Aversiveness of Strategies

Box 6.2   Prioritizing Ideas for Reducing Your Child's Target Behavior

Ethical Considerations

As at every step of the behavioral modification process, you need to think about the ethics of what you are doing. Behavioral modification should not be taken or undertaken lightly. Before you proceed, consider the following questions:

- Is changing the target behavior really going to help your child?
- Have you tried encouraging your child to perform the replacement behavior by using reinforcement?

- Is the strategy that you are going to use to reduce the target behavior going to cause more problems than it will solve?
- Could you get the same results by using less aversive strategies?
- Does your child understand why you are trying to change his behavior?

Final Plan

Take one final look at the thoughts that you have written down in this chapter. Weigh your options and check your gut feelings. In the lines below, write down how you are going to attempt to decrease the target behavior.

_____

_____

_____

Backup Plan

Take a few minutes to think of a backup plan, in case your first idea doesn't work. Follow the same process and write down what you come up with in the lines below. Have your backup plan use a different strategy than you used before. For instance, if your first attempt to teach your child a behavior that prevents the target behavior from occurring fails, your backup plan might involve a different method, such as rewarding a decrease in frequency.

_____

_____

_____

APPLYING WHAT YOU KNOW

There is certainly a lot to understand when developing behavioral modification programs that use punishment as a means of reducing inappropriate behavior (see figure 6.2). Take a few minutes to re-read the case

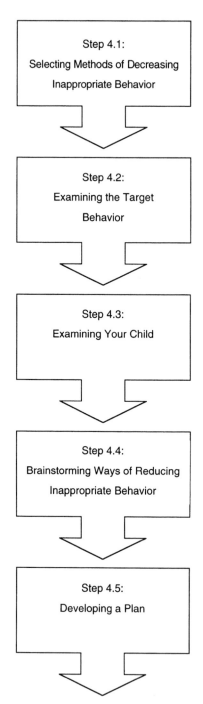

Figure 6.2   Flow Chart of Step 4

study at the beginning of the chapter. Then apply what you have learned in this chapter to the case study questions. We discuss each question below.

Question 1: When Developing a Behavioral Modification Program, What Problems Might Arise Because Gregory Has Mental Retardation?

As we have mentioned many times previously, behavioral modification is wrought with all kinds of ethical dilemmas. The process that is being outlined in this book could easily be abused if the needs of the child are not considered at all times. This is especially true when the child whose behavior you are trying to change has a disability, such as mental retardation.

In addition to the ethical dilemmas, attempting to change the behavior of children with mental retardation also presents parents and educators with many challenges. What challenges can you imagine Gregory's parents and teachers will have? What would you do to address these challenges?

Perhaps the biggest challenge when working with Gregory is to help him realize what is going on. He may not understand why he is being forced to wear a helmet. Nor might he understand that his behavior is associated with consequences. This could explain why reinforcement did not work.

Getting children with mental retardation to understand that certain behavior is good and will be rewarded, and other behavior is bad and will be punished, is essential for any behavioral modification strategies to work. For Gregory to understand this, his parents and teachers will have to follow every behavior with a quick consequence. Timing and consistency are crucial. As soon as Gregory stops banging his head, he should be rewarded. Right when he starts banging his head, some sort of negative consequence should be implemented.

Question 2: What Behavior-Reducing Strategies Might Be Appropriate for Gregory?

In this chapter we discussed many different types of strategies that could reduce inappropriate behaviors. However, not all of these strategies are suitable for all situations. From what you know about Gregory, what strategies might be appropriate for his parents and teachers to use?

Of the strategies discussed in this chapter, promoting incompatible behaviors and presenting aversive stimuli would probably be your best bet. These strategies are the most likely to produce a quick result. Further, presenting an incompatible behavior would not require that the child understand what is going on. The trick, however, is to find a behavior that prevents Gregory from hitting his head.

Question 3: What Behavior-Reducing Strategies Would Not Be Appropriate for Gregory?

Of the behavior-reducing strategies covered in this chapter, several would not be appropriate in Gregory's situation. For instance, from what is written in the case study, it sounds as though Gregory's parents and teachers have already tried to teach him appropriate behavior by using reinforcement, so this strategy probably wouldn't work, at least initially. However, teaching Gregory how to express his frustrations without hitting himself should certainly be a long-term goal.

Because Gregory's behavior is so severe and potentially life-altering, you probably would not want to settle on reducing the inappropriate behavior, unless you can reduce it to such a degree that he only gently taps his head when he is upset. For the present, Gregory's parents and teachers probably want to stop the behavior completely. In this case, promoting a reduction of the inappropriate behavior would not be advantageous.

Response-cost programs can be very useful when trying to reduce inappropriate behavior. However, these programs are useful only if the child understands the link between the behavior and the cost. Although Gregory could certainly be taught this association, it would likely take some time. Unfortunately, for his own safety Gregory's self-abuse needs to stop as soon as possible. Consequently, response-cost probably would not be a good strategy for his situation.

The final strategy covered in this chapter involved making the inappropriate behavior nonreinforcing. This can be an excellent method for reducing or eliminating behaviors that are caused by seeking attention, such as telling jokes in class or throwing spitballs in class. Unfortunately, it would be very difficult to use this strategy to help Gregory. After all, making Gregory self-abuse more to make the behavior nonreinforcing could produce drastic results.

7

STEP 5: IMPLEMENTING AND EVALUATING BEHAVIOR MODIFICATION PROGRAMS

CHAPTER OBJECTIVES

By the time you complete this chapter, you should be able to:

- Identify designs for behavioral modification programs.
- Select a design to use to change your child's behavior.
- Implement your behavioral modification program.
- Evaluate your behavioral modification program.
- Determine what to do if your program does not work.

CASE STUDY OF ANNA TAR

For many months, Mr. and Mrs. Tar have been desperately trying to get their teenage daughter, Anna, to clean up after herself. Every time she left a plate in the living room they would yell at her. Every time she left an article of clothing in the bathroom they would tell her to pick it up and put it in the clothes hamper. They begged, pleaded, punished, and rewarded. Nothing seemed to work. Finally, the Tars decided to try something a little more systematic.

Over the course of one week, Mr. and Mrs. Tar put a check on a piece of paper every time they saw that Anna left something lying around. By the end of the week, they found that Anna had left 52 things lying around the house. They calculated that this averaged roughly 5.4 items per day.

After the week was over, the Tars implemented a behavioral modification plan. Specifically, every time Mr. and Mrs. Tar found something that Anna had left lying around, she would not be able to watch television for that night. They tried this approach for one week and then decided to evaluate their efforts. At the end of the intervention, the Tars sat around their kitchen table trying to decide whether their approach had had any effect.

"The house certainly seems tidier," Mrs. Tar said, looking around the kitchen.

"Yes," admitted Mr. Tar, "but there wasn't a day this week that she wasn't punished for leaving something around."

"So does that mean that we should try something else?" Mrs. Tar asked. "Or should we continue with what we are doing?

CASE STUDY QUESTIONS

After reading the case study and this chapter, you should be able to answer the following questions. We will return to the case study and discuss these questions at the end of the chapter.

Question 1: What kind of design did the Tars use?

Question 2: What is wrong about how the Tars conducted their baseline investigation?

Question 3: What could the Tars have done to make assessing their program more effective?

INTRODUCTION

Thus far, this book has covered the basics of understanding behavior and behavioral modification. You have also identified behaviors that you want to change and have speculated about their causes. By now, you should also have a formal plan for increasing appropriate behaviors and decreasing inappropriate behaviors.

This chapter gets to the very heart of the matter: how to implement and evaluate your plan. Much of what is presented will sound like common sense. For instance, if you implement your plan and the good behavior increases and the bad behavior decreases, you could guess that your plan was effective. But there is more to it than that, as you will soon see.

Without effective implementation, the best made plans are likely to fail. Further, without understanding whether or why your plan failed, you will not be able to revise your work and eventually become successful. Please remember that it may take you many tries to develop a behavioral modification program that works. So learn from your mistakes and from your child's behavior.

STEP 5.1: COLLECTING BASELINE DATA

Before you start implementing your plan, you will first need to collect baseline data. If you don't remember from chapter 1, baseline data are what you are going to use to see whether your child's behavior is improving. The data are a measure of how frequently your child is performing the target behavior or how intense the target behavior is before you do anything about it.

You should have collected baseline data as part of chapter 4. Otherwise it would have been difficult for you to develop a hypothesis about the behavior's cause. If you have not collected baseline data, go back to chapter 4 and do so before proceeding.

The key to remember is that you need to continue taking data the same way throughout this entire step. So however you gathered baseline data should be the same method you use to collect data after you intervene. Otherwise you will not be able to determine whether the behavior is improving due to the intervention or to changes in data collection procedures.

TYPES OF PROGRAM DESIGNS

Okay, so you have baseline data on your child's target behavior. Now you need to figure out what design to use when implementing your program.

There are several to choose from. Each has various strengths and weaknesses. Although there is an infinite number or combination of designs, we only cover four common ones:

- AB designs
- ABA designs
- ABAB designs
- ABC designs

AB Designs

The first thing you are probably wondering is, "What is up with the As and the Bs!" Good question! "As" stand for times when the behavior is being measured but nothing is being done to change it. For example, when data are graphed, baselines are designated with an "A." "Bs" on the other hand indicate that something has been done to change the behavior. If you look at figure 7.1, the section marked with an "A" indicates how the child was doing without any interventions, and "B" indicates how the child is doing with the intervention in place. A solid line is usually used to show where the baseline ends and where the intervention phase begins.

Figure 7.1 graphs data on a child who is swearing. Before her parents intervened, she was swearing 14 to 17 times per day (see the section labeled "A" on the graph). Then the parents implemented some sort of behavioral modification program (note the line in between days

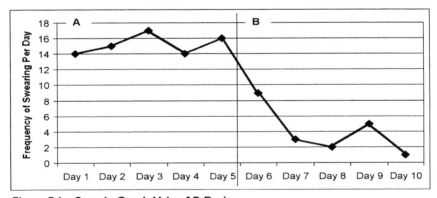

Figure 7.1   Sample Graph Using AB Design

5 and 6). For example, the parents could have implemented a response-cost program in which the child lost 10 minutes of television time every time she swore. The section of the graph to the right of the line indicates how frequently the target behavior occurred after the intervention was put into place (see the section labeled "B" on the graph).

Strengths of AB designs.   One of the strengths of AB designs is that they are relatively easy to implement. All you have to do is collect baseline data and then implement your strategies. Further, AB designs are the beginning part of all the designs that we discuss in this chapter. Once you implement an AB design, you can always change to form other designs.

Weaknesses of AB designs.   One of the problems of AB designs is that you can never be certain what is causing the change in behavior. For example, maybe your child's friends told her that swearing wasn't cool, or there is a new trendy word to use and that is why she isn't swearing as much as she used to.

Further, with AB designs, the intervention never ends. This might be fine for situations where the intervention is using natural reinforcers, such as feelings of accomplishment. But in most cases you will eventually need to end the program. After all, it is unlikely that you will still be paying your child to clean her room when she is 30 years old!

ABA Designs

The first "A" on a data graph is usually the data collected during baseline. The "B" is data collected while the intervention is being implemented. What does the last "A" signify?

The second "A" is called a "reversal." Basically, this means that you have reverted back to what you did before you intervened, which is nothing. You can also consider the second A as a second baseline.

As discussed previously, one of the primary weaknesses of the AB design is that the child is always on some sort of behavioral modification program. Having a second "A" allows you to determine whether the change in behavior has become internalized. That is, did what you do sink in? Or would the behavior return to normal when the modification program is over?

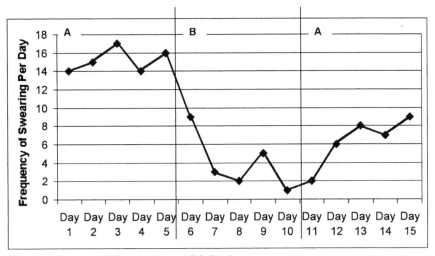

Figure 7.2 Sample Graph Using ABA Design

Look at figure 7.2. The parents of the swearing child stopped implementing their behavior change program between the tenth and eleventh day. The area of the graph marked with the second "A" (i.e., reversal) shows what happened after the intervention ceased. By comparing the behavior during the second "A" with the first, you can determine whether the child has internalized the behavior; that is, you can see whether the behavior has become naturally reinforced.

Strengths of ABA designs.   The main strength of ABA designs is that you have a better idea of whether the intervention actually affected the behavior. Clearly, if the behavior changes when the intervention is implemented (B) and then returns to baseline levels when the intervention ends, chances are the intervention is responsible.

Weaknesses of ABA designs.   The main weakness of ABA designs is that they shouldn't be used in all cases. Specifically, if you cannot risk the target behavior returning to normal, then ABA designs are not for you. For example, if you were trying to reduce unsafe or violent behavior, why would you risk having the behavior return to the way it was before you intervened?

ABAB Designs

You can probably figure out what the ABAB design is. It is just like the ABA design; however, the intervention is implemented for a second time (see figure 7.3). So imagine that your child is swearing; you collect baseline data and attempt to learn about the behavior's cause. Based on what you know about the behavior, you have decided to create some sort of intervention, which you implement for a while before stopping and then restarting it.

Why would you stop the intervention? There could be many reasons. For example, maybe you wanted to see whether the behavior had changed for good. After all, you can't always follow your child around rewarding appropriate behavior and punishing inappropriate behavior. Or maybe you wanted to see whether the intervention really had some effect on the behavior. After all, if the behavior goes back to normal right after you stopped the intervention, you can conclude that it was the intervention that caused the initial change.

Strengths of ABAB designs.   As discussed previously, the ABAB design is very useful when you want to make sure that the intervention is causing the change in behavior. Think about it. What are the chances of something else changing the behavior twice exactly at the moment when you stop the intervention? Using ABAB designs would be an excellent way of determining whether your reinforcers or punishers are truly reinforcing and punishing from your child's perspective.

Weakness of ABAB designs.   As with ABA designs, the primary problem with ABAB designs is that they are not appropriate for target behaviors that shouldn't be allowed to return to normal, such as those that are aggressive or self-abusive. Further, these designs can be some-

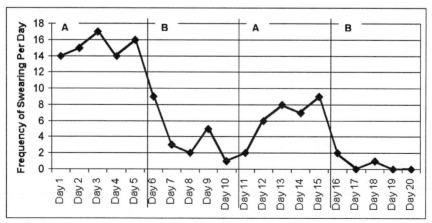

Figure 7.3 Sample Graph Using ABAB Design

what time consuming to use. You have to collect baseline data, then intervene, then stop the intervention, then start the intervention again.

ABC Designs

By now you should have a good handle on what "As" and "Bs" are, but what do you think "C" is? Let's suppose that you are a parent of the child we have been discussing, the one who keeps swearing. Let us also suppose that you collected baseline just like the data presented in figures 7.1 to 7.3 and that you implemented a strategy to change the behavior. Unfortunately, the strategy didn't work (see figure 7.4). In fact, it actually increased the inappropriate behavior. So you want to try something new.

The "C" in ABC represents a second intervention. And if that intervention didn't work, you could add a third and fourth strategy. Your design would then be an ABCDE. In other words, each non-"A" letter denotes a brand new attempt at changing the behavior.

You could even throw in a few periods where you don't try anything (i.e., "A"). For example, you might try the first strategy (i.e. "B"); that would be written as AB. But that strategy didn't work, so you went back to the drawing board and didn't try anything for a while—ABA. Then

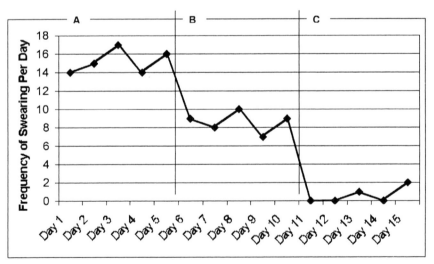

Figure 7.4   Sample Graph Using ABC

you thought of a new way of reducing your child's swearing, so you tried that—ABAC. That didn't work either, so you took another break where you didn't try anything—ABACA. Get the picture? You literally have an infinite number of designs depending on how many interventions you are willing to try.

Strengths of ABC designs.   The biggest strength of ABC designs is that they allow you to implement multiple strategies. Further, you can gradually fade strategies so that your child doesn't become dependent on them. For instance, for the first intervention (B), you could reward your child with 20 minutes of free time for every time he performs the desired behavior. For the second intervention (C), you could drop the reward to 15 minutes. Then for the third intervention (D), you could reduce it further to 10 minutes. And so on.

Weaknesses of ABC designs.   The main weakness of ABC designs is that they could be confusing for your child. Imagine that your parents tried to change your behavior. They did one thing one week and then another the next week and then something completely different a few weeks later. Not only might you become confused, you might think to yourself, "Why should I care? They are just going to change what is going to happen in a few days."

STEP 5.2: SELECTING A PROGRAM DESIGN

Now that you understand the various program designs, it is time for you to select one to implement with your child. Go back and look at your target behavior. Think about the reinforcers and punishers that you developed in chapters 5 and 6. Do any of the designs that we have discussed match your individuals needs?

Of course you could start with a simple AB design in which you collect baseline data and then implement the reward and punishment program that you developed. Then, if the program doesn't seem to work, you can try implementing the backup plans that you listed in chapters 5 and 6—which would become an ABC design.

Keep in mind that no matter what design you choose, your end goal is to have your child perform the desired behavior independently from your program. That is, when the program stops, the behavior will continue. So you may want to think about developing a behavioral modification program with a design that slowly fades away the reinforcers and punishers. You might use an ABCDE design where the B, C, D, and E are all variations of the same intervention. For instance, the B could signify constant reinforcement. C could involve a ratio reinforcement schedule in which every two appropriate behaviors are rewarded. For D you could reinforce the appropriate behavior every four times it occurs. And so on. The idea is that, before you start, you have a general idea how your program is going to be implemented.

STEP 5.3: IMPLEMENTING YOUR PROGRAM

By now, you should have a specific design and strategy in mind. Moreover, you are probably anxious to begin implementing your program. Before you do, there are several things to consider, including

- consistency,
- formative evaluation, and
- knowing when to change.

Consistency

Perhaps the most important factor when implementing a behavioral modification program is to be consistent. This means that you have to reinforce the behaviors the way you said you were going to reinforce them and punish the behaviors in the way you said you were going to punish them. This is particularly important when your child is very young or has mental retardation. After all, the child may not know what is going on, so if you are inconsistent in what you do, it will take him or her much longer to figure out what you are trying to do.

In addition to being consistent in how you implement your plan, you must be consistent in how you measure your child's behavior. If you change how you are defining the behavior or recording data, you could be affecting how frequently the behavior appears to be occurring. Consequently you may not be able to tell whether your intervention is actually helping or hurting.

Formative Evaluation

Formative evaluation means that you are evaluating what is happening as you go. Often as you are trying to change your child's behavior you will realize that something isn't going to work or that something may work better. You may even want to change what the target behavior is.

Although it is important to be consistent, it is also important to constantly check to see what effect you are having. After all, you do not want to keep doing something that is making the situation worse. For example, suppose that you want your child to clean his room, so you develop a reward and punishment system. Perhaps you pay him a dollar if he cleans his room and you prevent him from going to the movies if he doesn't. However, you quickly realize that the dollar doesn't entice your child into performing the desired behavior (e.g., it is too little money) and he doesn't care whether he goes to the movies or not (e.g., there is nothing that he wants to see). In a situation like this, you may have to make a change in your behavioral modification plan to be successful. Without evaluating your success as you go, you wouldn't have realized that the original plan wasn't working.

Knowing When to Change

As discussed previously, being consistent is essential to be successful in changing your child's behavior. But so is knowing when to change. Does that sound confusing? Think about the example described previously, where the child gets a dollar for cleaning his room and does not get to go to the movies if he doesn't clean his room. In this situation it probably is clear that you might either want to increase the reward for the desired behavior or change the punishment to something that matters to your child. However, knowing when to change and when to stand fast is not as easy as it sounds. Consider the following examples.

Often children will react negatively to your attempt to change their behavior. Have you ever seen children throw temper tantrums? How do children usually react if a parent doesn't give them what they want? They usually demand what they want, maybe kick and scream. If parents change their approach and give the children what they want, the parents are actually making the situation worse by promoting the inappropriate behavior. After all, kids aren't stupid. If they see that they can get their way by yelling and throwing things, they will keep using this strategy.

Is this to say that parents should never give in to a temper tantrum? Well, it depends. Imagine that you were on a plane and your child was screaming. For the sake of the other passengers on board, this might be a good time to give the child what she wants to quiet her down. In other words, sometimes it is appropriate to change a plan temporarily. (We discuss dealing specifically with temper tantrums in chapter 9.)

Since we have talked about different types of research designs, you have probably been thinking, "Okay, when do I stop taking baseline data and start my intervention?" or "When do I shift from a 'B' to an 'A' or a 'C'?" These are excellent questions.

When changing from a baseline to intervention, intervention to intervention (e.g., "B" to "C"), or intervention to reversals (e.g., a second "A"), you need to keep two things in mind. The first is the trend of the data. The second is the longevity of the data.

Trend of data. The trend of data indicates whether the frequency of the behavior is increasing, decreasing, or staying the same. Whenever possible, you want to intervene when the baseline data are stable or going in the opposite direction from what you want. For example, suppose that you want to increase the amount of homework that your child turns in complete and on time. You collect some baseline data and graph them (see figure 7.5).

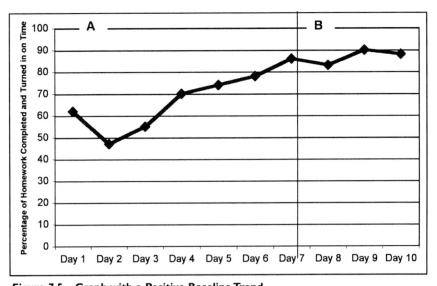

Figure 7.5   Graph with a Positive Baseline Trend

Look at the data graphed in figure 7.5. Notice the trend of the child's behavior? As you can see from the baseline (A), the behavior is improving without any intervention. We don't know for sure, but it would seem that the behavior would have continued to improve even if the intervention had never been implemented. In a situation such as this, you probably would not want do anything.

Now look at figure 7.6. In this scenario, the trend is actually downward. That is to say, the child is turning in less and less homework over time. Since you are trying to increase the behavior, you could intervene even though the behavior is not stable. If the behavior starts to increase after your intervention, then you can surmise that you are having a positive effect on the target behavior.

You might be thinking to yourself, "But what do I do if there is no trend to the baseline data?" This is a very good question since behavior is frequently chaotic. For example, consider the data presented in figure 7.7. Sometimes the student turns in his homework on time and other times he doesn't. His behavior appears completely random. It is all over the place. Can you intervene?

Because your goal would be to get your child to turn in his homework on time consistently, yes—you can intervene when the baseline is chaotic. Basically, you can intervene anytime the baseline is different

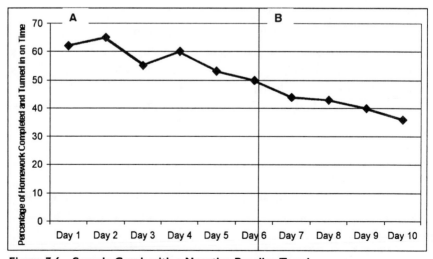

Figure 7.6   Sample Graph with a Negative Baseline Trend

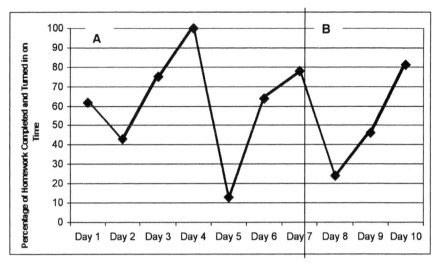

Figure 7.7   Sample Graph with Random Baseline Data

from what you want the end product to be. So even though the child in figure 7.7 does turn in his homework some of the time, his behavior is not yet where you want it to be.

Longevity of data.   In addition to looking at the data's trend, you need to also think about how long you have been collecting data, or their longevity. For instance, you don't want to base your decision to intervene, or change interventions, on one or two data points because you won't be able to get an accurate picture of what is going on. Imagine that you are trying to get your child to turn in all of his homework on time and you stop intervening as soon as he turns in his homework once. You don't know if the behavior is going to continue to the next day or the next week, which is your goal.

So how long should you collect baseline data before you implement your program? Well, it depends. Clearly if the target behavior was extremely important and needed to be changed right away you might implement a program as soon as possible. But generally you don't want to do anything until you have a good idea whether the behavior is increasing, decreasing, or staying the same. So you might need to collect data five times. Or you might need to collect data 50 times. It all depends on your situation.

STEP 5.4: EVALUATING YOUR PROGRAM

As discussed in the previous section, evaluation is a very important part of the behavioral modification process. Without evaluating what you are doing, you will have no idea whether your efforts are bearing fruit. Further, evaluation occurs throughout the behavioral modification process. For instance, you evaluate your child's behavior before you intervene (i.e., while you gather baseline data). You also evaluate the program as you go.

Evaluation is more than simply seeing if the behavior has changed to the degree that you want it to change. Evaluating your program will help you fine tune it so that it is more effective. For instance, you might find that behavior is not occurring when and where you thought it was, so you have to adjust how you are measuring or recording the behavior.

Evaluation can also help you learn more about your child. For example, you might find that the cause of your child's behavior is not what you first guessed but something completely different. Maybe your child has an undiagnosed disability. Or maybe she is willfully disobeying you.

Evaluation is as much an art as it is a skill. It is difficult to teach people the analytic skills that truly exceptional evaluators have. However, in this chapter we cover some of the basics, such as methods for graphing data and applied behavior analysis.

Graphing Results

Graphs are wonderful ways of looking at a whole bunch of data all at once. By scanning one visual snapshot you can get a good idea of what is happening. Line graphs are particularly useful because they show the behavior over time, which is necessary to determine if you are being successful.

When using graphs it is customary to have the horizontal axis, also called the X-axis, represent the passage of time. Perhaps you can list each day that you collected data or each trial where you observed to see whether the behavior occurred. The Y-axis, or vertical line to the side of the graph, usually represents the behavior.

At times you might want to have two separate graphs. You could have one for the target behavior that you are trying to decrease and one for the replacement behavior that you are trying to increase. Placing the graphs side-by-side enables you to compare both behaviors at once.

Figuring Out What the Data Means

Graphing data makes evaluating what you have done much easier, but it is not the end of the process. You now have to interpret the results. It takes a lot of hard work and insight to be able to interpret data effectively. Although teaching you the needed skills is beyond the scope of this book, some practice would be beneficial. In this section we review several groups of data. Let's see what you can make of them.

Take a look at the data presented in figure 7.8. First of all, what kind of design was used? Was it successful?

The design used in figure 7.8 is an ABA design, which means baseline data were gathered, the intervention was implemented, and then the intervention was taken away. Do you think that the intervention worked? Why? What would you have done differently?

The first thing that you might notice is that the baseline is constant, which is good, but it is short. Data were only gathered three times. Al-

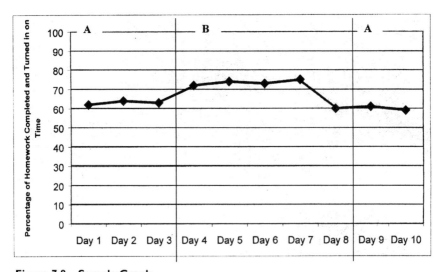

Figure 7.8   Sample Graph

though this might be fine for behaviors that need to be changed right away, such as those that are life-threatening, usually you will need more than three data points to determine the behavior's trend. It could very well be that the behavior would have improved without any intervention.

The second thing that you probably noticed was that the target behavior increased in frequency after the intervention was introduced. As just discussed, due to the short baseline, we cannot tell for sure whether this change was directly the result of the intervention. However, there is something else to consider. Did the target behavior improve enough? Of course this is up to the parents of the child to decide, but keep in mind that just because a behavior improves, it doesn't mean that you are done intervening. If the parents of the child depicted in the graph want to increase the behavior further, they might want to alter their intervention a little bit. Perhaps they could change the reinforcer. If they did this, they would add a section to the graph and label it "C."

Now look at figure 7.9. Here we have two graphs, one that illustrates the target behavior, and another that shows the replacement behavior. What can you tell from studying these graphs?

What did you learn by looking at the graphs presented in figure 7.9? For starters, the baselines look good. The trends are conducive for starting an intervention. They both show trends different from what you would expect after an intervention has been implemented. They are also long enough to make a reasonable prediction about the behaviors had the interventions not occurred.

From the graph on the top, it would appear that the intervention is having a dramatic effect on the target behavior. Specifically, whatever the parents are doing is really increasing the child's study time. But what about the graph that follows, the one that shows percentage of homework completed on time? What does that tell you?

From the data graphed on the bottom, it would appear that the first intervention (B) had very little effect on the amount of homework completed. Moreover, the second intervention (C) seemed to have a negative effect on the completion of homework since the percent of homework completed actually went down. But what does all of this information mean?

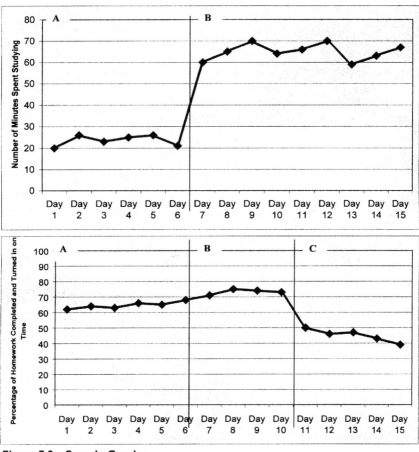

Figure 7.9   Sample Graphs

One thing that you might conclude from the data presented in figure 7.9 is that an increase in study time does not automatically translate to homework being completed. But why? Think about it. How is the target behavior in the left-hand graph (i.e., time spent studying) defined? We don't really know, but it probably has something to do with the amount of time sitting at a desk with a book open. Does this mean that the child is actually studying? No. She could be sitting there staring blankly at the book and not doing anything. If this were true, you might want to rethink how you define and measure "studying." In fact, you might want to forget about measuring the length of time studying and start focusing on the quality of time studying, such as measuring the number of problems or assignments the child does correctly.

Another interpretation of these data is that, as time goes on, the homework assignments are getting harder and harder. So the decrease in homework completed is not related to the amount of time spent studying but to the level of difficulty of the work. In other words, the target behavior (i.e., completing homework assignments) is not necessarily the result of willful choice but the product of the child's ability to understand the assignments. If this were true, you would want to change your approach to the problem. Instead of encouraging the student to complete the work, you would want to get her the help she needs so that she can learn how to do it. After all, no matter what punishers or reinforcers you use, if she can't do the work, she will not complete the assignments.

STEP 5.5: FIGURING OUT WHY THE INTERVENTION DIDN'T WORK

After looking at all the available data, you might still be wondering why your behavioral modification program didn't work. Don't get discouraged. As mentioned in the first chapter, changing how somebody behaves is not as easy as it sounds. If you were less than successful this time, consider the following and then try again.

Expectations Too High

The first thing that you might consider when trying to figure out why your program didn't change your child's behavior is your expectations. Are you expecting too much from your child? Are you wanting your child to change too quickly? Maybe, developmentally, your child is just not ready to do what you are asking.

Wrong Hypothesis

Another explanation of why your behavioral modification program did not work could involve the cause of the target behavior. It could be that the target behavior was caused by something completely different from you originally thought. Maybe your child can't help but perform the target behavior. Maybe he has a condition like dyslexia and simply can't write letters correctly all of the time or has a lot of problems reading. Go back to chapter 4 and reevaluate the information you have gathered.

Wrong Reinforcer or Punisher

Next, you might want to think about the reinforcers or punishers that you used. Maybe your child didn't think that the reinforcers were reinforcing. Maybe from your child's perspective, you saying "good job" was really a punishment. The same could be true for the punishers that you used. After all, maybe being sent to her room was exactly what your daughter wanted.

Another explanation is that the reinforcers and punishers you selected were not powerful enough. Maybe your child liked having you say "good job," but she was unwilling to work really hard just to hear those words. Maybe being sent to her room wasn't a good thing in your daughter's eyes, but it was better than eating her broccoli. Perhaps your strategy would be more effective if you retooled how you reinforced the appropriate behavior and punished the inappropriate behavior.

Your Execution of the Program

Another potential explanation why your program didn't work could lie with how you executed it. Maybe you didn't keep at it long enough. Maybe you were inconsistent. Maybe you were not clear about your expectations or what the consequences of various behaviors were.

STEP 5.6: GOING BACK TO THE DRAWING BOARD

If you found that your intervention didn't work as well as you would have liked, you might consider redeveloping your program. Go back and look at your ideas for backup reinforcers and punishers in chapters 5 and 6. Maybe it is time to give them a try. Or maybe you want to start over completely. This latter option is particularly useful if you have to rethink the cause of the behavior or identify an entirely new behavior on which to focus.

APPLYING WHAT YOU HAVE READ

This chapter addresses many issues regarding how to implement and evaluate your behavioral modification program (see figure 7.10). Now let's apply what you have learned. Go back and read the case study at the beginning of the chapter, then answer the related questions. We discuss them below.

Question 1: What Kind of Design Did the Tars Use?

This chapter covered many different designs for behavioral modification programs. Each design has its advantages and disadvantages. Understanding which design is best for your situation will help you develop the best program possible.

Go back and read the case study at the beginning of the chapter. What kind of design did the Tars use with their daughter Anna? What are some of the strengths of this design? What are some of the weaknesses?

From what is written in the case study, it looks like Mr. and Mrs. Tar collected baseline data and then intervened. This could be an AB design. However, it is unclear whether they kept gathering data after they stopped intervening. If they did, their design would have been an ABA.

One of the strengths of these designs is that they are relatively easy to implement. You simply gather information about the behavior, then do something to change the behavior. The main problem of these designs is that you can never be sure if your intervention caused the change or some other factor did.

Question 2: What Is Wrong About How the Tars Conducted Their Baseline Investigation?

We have discussed compiling baseline data in several chapters. It is a very important component of the behavioral change process. Not only can baseline data help you determine the cause of the behavior, but they are also used to see if the target behavior has been affected. Consequently, you will need to do a good job collecting baseline data if you want to be successful in changing your child's behavior.

Figure 7.10   Flow Chart of Step 5

How did the Tars develop the baseline on Anna's target behavior? What did they do wrong? What could they have done differently?

When the Tars developed the baseline, they put a check on a piece of paper for every time Anna left something lying around the house. This is fine. If you recall from chapter 4, this is frequency recording.

Unfortunately, the Tars clumped all of their baseline data together. They simply totaled the number of items that Anna left around during the entire week. This isn't a good idea because the Tars cannot see the behavior's trend. They cannot tell if the behavior's frequency is increasing or decreasing. It might have been that Anna was actually getting neater on her own and that she would have decreased the target behavior.

Question 3: What Could the Tars Have Done to Make Assessing Their Program More Effective?

If you cannot effectively assess your behavioral modification plan, all of your efforts could be in vain. That seems to be the problem the Tars are facing. They have no idea whether they should continue their program or try something new. What could they have done better?

In addition to collecting baseline data for each day, as discussed above, the Tars should have continued collecting data during their intervention. They then could have compared the number of items left around the house during the intervention to the number of items left during baseline. This would have helped them determine whether Anna was getting neater.

STRATEGIES FOR MODIFYING
VARIOUS BEHAVIORS

CHAPTER OBJECTIVE

By the time you complete this chapter, you should be able to:

• Identify strategies for modifying various behaviors.

CASE STUDY OF PERRY NOLE

Perry is a student in elementary school. He has been diagnosed with attention deficit hyperactivity disorder (ADHD) and frequently gets out of his seat to talk to other students. Whenever his teacher tells him to get back to his seat and stop talking, Perry willingly does what he is told. However, his appropriate behavior does not last long. Within a couple of minutes he is out of his seat again and talking to somebody.

"That is it!" Perry's teacher yelled. "Go to time out!"

Perry looked back at her with startled eyes. "I am sorry," he said sincerely. "It won't happen again." He quickly retraced his steps and sat down quietly in his chair.

"I said go to time out!" his teacher insisted.

Perry looked around at his classmates, who all looked back at him and shrugged.

"What is 'time out'?" Perry asked meekly.

The teacher flinched a little and looked around the room. Grabbing a nearby chair, she faced it to the corner of the walls.

"Here," she said. "Sit here."

"For how long?"

"Until I tell you that you can return to your seat."

Slowly, Perry got up, gathered his books and papers, and began walking to the corner of the room where the chair waited for him.

"Leave your belongings behind," the teacher said. "You are going to sit here and think about what you have done. And if you get up before I tell you or make any noise at all, you will be sent to the principal's office and be given detention."

Needless to say, a minute later Perry was walking down the hall toward the principal's office.

CASE STUDY QUESTIONS

After reading the case study and this chapter, you should be able to answer the following questions. We will return to the case study and discuss these questions at the end of the chapter.

Question 1: Why didn't this strategy work?
Question 2: How could self-monitoring or self-questioning have worked in Perry's situation?
Question 3: Other than trying to change Perry's behavior, what else could the teacher have done?

INTRODUCTION

By now, you should have a good understanding of behavioral modification and the processes for changing your child's behavior. However, you might need some ideas to help you put everything together. For example, you might need help developing a token economy system. Or you might need to learn more about when to use time outs. In this chapter we discuss many strategies, including:

- Token economies
- Behavioral contracts
- Chaining
- Time outs
- Modeling
- System of least restrictive prompts
- Redirection
- Direct instruction
- Self-monitoring
- Self-questioning

These are just some of the strategies that you might find useful when trying to improve your child's behaviors. For more ideas, check with teaching organizations and resources. You should be able to find a number of them on the Internet.

TOKEN ECONOMIES

Token economies are very popular behavioral modification strategies. They involve setting up a system in which children can earn artificial reinforcers if they perform the desired behaviors. The reinforcers can be anything from checks on a board to pieces of make believe money. These reinforcers are then traded in for something the child wants.

The key to token economies is that the reinforcers have to be desired by the child. Further, the rate of exchange between the tokens and the reinforcers must be reasonable. For example, imagine that you got a poker chip every time you showed up to work early. Moreover, you could "buy" vacation days with the chips that you accumulate. Unfortunately, for every hour of vacation, you need one million chips! Would this system encourage you to perform the desired behavior (i.e., show up for work early)? Probably not. After all, it is too difficult to get rewarded.

Token economies can also be used as part of a response-cost program. For example, suppose that you had a poker chip taken away every time you showed up late for work. Assuming that you want to keep your chips, this could motivate you to be on time.

Again, when using token economies to decrease behaviors, you have to be careful not to have inappropriate behaviors be too costly. Imagine that you were late 10 seconds for work and your boss took away 50 chips! Although such penalties might strongly encourage you to be on time, you could dig such a hole for yourself that you could never save enough tokens to get rewarded. If that were the case, would you bother trying to earn the reward?

Another key to using token economies is to catch the child when she is doing something good. Reward positive behavior frequently. An overemphasis on taking away the currency will diminish the strategy's appeal and reduce its effectiveness.

BEHAVIORAL CONTRACTS

Behavioral contracts are also very common strategies for modifying behavior. The general idea is that you and your child get together, discuss each other's expectations, and come to an agreement about how you are going to handle the situation. Behavioral contracts typically include the following components:

- The behavior to be performed (including when, where, how often, etc.)
- What will happen if the behavior is performed
- What will happen if the behavior is not performed

It is important to involve the child in the development of behavioral contracts. The child's participation in the contract's development is likely to help motivate him to comply with the agreement. Further, having the child help write up the contract will ensure that he understands what is expected of him and what will happen if he does not follow through on his end of the deal.

Behavioral contracts can be used in tandem with other strategies, such as token economies. For instance, a behavioral contract might stipulate that if the child does such and such behavior, she will get three to-kens. Further, if she saves up 10 tokens, she will be rewarded with a pre-determined outcome.

Figure 8.1 presents a sample behavioral contract. When creating your own form, have some fun with it. Make it look very legal and formal. Perhaps have witnesses and a signing ceremony.

CHAINING

Chaining is a term for strategies that involve teaching somebody each step needed to complete a task. There are two types of chaining, back-ward and forward. Backward chaining is when you teach the last step first and progressively work your way backward so that the child learns all of the tasks. Forward chaining is when you teach your child the first step in a task, then the second, and the third, and so on until all the steps are mastered.

To illustrate how to use backward and forward chaining, imagine that you are going to teach your child how to make a pizza. Before teaching, you break the task down into several broad steps:

- Step 1: Make the dough
- Step 2: Spread the dough on a pan
- Step 3: Put sauce on top of the dough
- Step 4: Put cheese on top of the sauce
- Step 5: Put pizza in the oven

If you were using forward chaining to teach your child how to make pizzas, you would begin with the first step. When he mastered the first step, he would go on to the second step. After he mastered the second step, he would move on to the third step, and so on until he could make a pizza.

If you were using backward chaining, you would complete the first four steps and then have your child complete the last step. Once she masters that step, you would do the first three steps and then have her complete the last two steps. Once she mastered those steps, you would do the first two steps and she would complete the last three steps, and so on until she could complete all of the steps.

Behavioral Contract

It is agreed that if Billy Kramer:

- ✓ Takes the garbage cans to the curb each Monday night
- ✓ Brings the empty garbage cans back to the garage each Tuesday afternoon
- ✓ Feeds the dog two cups of dog food each morning before he goes to school
- ✓ Fills the dog's water dish each morning before he goes to school and whenever it is empty
- ✓ Walks the dog around the block each night before he goes to bed

Each week he will earn his choice of the following:

- ✓ A pizza with his favorite toppings
- ✓ The right to stay up one hour past his regular bed time
- ✓ Five dollars to be applied to the purchase of a new computer game

If Billy does not complete the assigned tasks at the appointed times, he will lose the privilege of:

- ✓ Watching television for one day
- ✓ Using the computer
- ✓ Going out with his friend on the weekend

Signed: _____   _____   _____

           Judy Kramer   Warren Kramer   Billy Kramer

Effective Date: _____

Termination Date: _____

Figure 8.1   An Example of a Completed Behavioral Contract

TIME OUTS

Time out is a strategy frequently used for disruptive behavior. Basically, when a child is being inappropriate the parent or teacher sends the child to a designated area, such as a corner or time out room, where the child sits in isolation for so many minutes. After the allotted time, the child comes back to wherever he or she was before the time out.

Although time out is used as a punishment, it frequently is not. Just imagine if you wanted to leave the classroom and your teacher sent you to time out because of your behavior. Time out then would be a reinforcer for inappropriate behavior. For this reason, time outs are often criticized.

Another concern about time outs is that they do not teach the child how to behave. They are simply a way of de-escalating problematic behavior. They also give the teacher or parent some time to regroup.

If you are going to use time outs as part of your behavioral modification strategy, you should keep the follow guidelines in mind:

- Keep time outs to a reasonable length of time: no more than five minutes for children who are hyperactive, no more than fifteen for other children.
- Warn the child ahead of time that he will earn a time out if that specific behavior continues.
- After the time out is over, discuss with your child what she did wrong and what she should have done instead.
- Time outs should be used after all else has failed.
- Use time outs sparingly.
- Use time outs in conjunction with a reinforcer for appropriate behavior.
- The child in time out should be monitored at all times.
- The time out environment should be free from hazardous materials or playthings.

MODELING

Modeling is a strategy by which children are shown how to perform a certain task. But it is more than simply demonstrating the necessary steps. It involves talking through the thought process that is used to complete the task. For instance, if you were teaching your child how to calculate addition problems, you would not only show her how to solve the problem, you would explain each step. Moreover, you should explain why you didn't do certain things, such as why you didn't start adding left to right.

SYSTEM OF LEAST RESTRICTIVE PROMPTS

The system of least restrictive prompts is a systematic strategy whereby children are taught steps of a task and the amount of assistance that they are given is gradually faded. For example, suppose that you are teaching your child how to write the alphabet. You might use the following levels of prompts:

- **Full physical prompt:** You take your child by the hand and physically make her write the letters.
- **Partial physical prompt:** You guide your child's hand to where it needs to go.
- **Gestural prompt:** You point to the paper where the child should be writing.
- **Direct verbal prompt:** You tell your child what to do (e.g., "Now cross your 'T'.").
- **Indirect verbal prompt:** You give your child a subtle verbal hint (e.g., "What should you do now?").

The idea behind the system of least restrictive prompts is that you use the level of prompt that employs the least amount of support your child needs. Further, you gradually fade the amount of support over time. So you might begin by using full physical prompts and then fade to a partial physical and so on until your child can complete the task without any support.

You can even combine prompts. For instance, you might point to the paper and then say, "Write a letter 'A'." This would be a gestural prompt (i.e., pointing to the paper) and a direct verbal prompt (i.e., telling your child what to do).

REDIRECTION

Redirection is often an effective strategy for de-escalating inappropriate behavior. The key is to get the child distracted from whatever is triggering the behavior. For example, suppose that your child is upset because somebody called him a silly name. You can see that the event is really bothering him, and the more he thinks about it, the madder he gets. Rather than letting him get angrier and angrier, you might consider getting his mind off what happened by giving him something else to think about. Maybe ask him where he wants to go for his summer vacation. Or ask him about the movie he just saw. Anything that could divert his attention would work.

Redirection is also commonly used for children who are hyperactive. When you see that your child is having difficulty sitting still, try giving her something active to do. Teachers can have their students run errands or hand out papers. Parents could have children help with making dinner or run around the yard.

When using redirection it is important to catch the behavior before it is firmly underway. You should look for triggers to potential behaviors and telltale signs, such as a child starting to get frustrated. Then redirect the child using something positive. If you try to redirect using a negative, such as by saying, "If you don't stop your crying, I will give you something to cry about," then the behavior is likely to continue to escalate.

DIRECT INSTRUCTION

Direct instruction is a teaching strategy that has been found to be very effective for many children. It consists of six steps:

- Step 1: Review prior lessons
- Step 2: Present new content
- Step 3: Provide structured, teacher-guided practice
- Step 4: Provide immediate correction
- Step 5: Provide independent practice
- Step 6: Review

Direct instruction is typically used to help students acquire academic skills, such as learning math. Basically, the teacher would review what has been covered before, present new content, and then provide highly structured, teacher-guided practice. For instance, the teacher may make the entire class repeat after him, "2+2 = 4, 2+3 = 5, 2+4 = 6" and so on. The teacher would correct any errors immediately and then provide independent practices, such as through worksheets or exams. The content would then be reviewed the next day.

SELF-MONITORING

Unlike direct instruction, self-monitoring is a child-centered strategy. It involves having the child keep track of her progress on various academic and nonacademic tasks. For example, the child might graph her performance on spelling quizzes or how many times she got out of her chair without asking.

Self-monitoring tends to be very motivating for children. In addition, since they are participating in the behavioral modification process, the strategy can also be empowering. However, perhaps its biggest advantage is that making a child think about her own behavior might improve the behavior without any further intervention.

SELF-QUESTIONING

Self-questioning is a form of self-monitoring. When using this strategy, a child will ask himself a series of questions about his own behavior. For instance, if he is working on a writing assignment, a child might think, "Did I capitalize everything that needs to be capitalized? Did I double check my spelling?" A child who is working on her social skills might think, "Am I making eye contact? Am I dominating the conversation?"

Not only does self-questioning give children valuable self-reflection skills, but it also makes children take responsibility for their own actions. Further, as with other self-monitoring techniques, the implementation of self-questioning could be an effective method for changing behavior. Also like other self-monitoring strategies, self-questioning tends to be effective only with children who have the cognitive ability to understand how and when to use it.

APPLYING WHAT YOU HAVE READ

In this chapter we discussed several strategies that might help you improve your child's behavior. Now let's apply what you have read. Go back and read the case study at the beginning of the chapter. Then try to answer the following questions.

Question 1: Why Didn't This Strategy Work?

Perry's teacher implemented a time out strategy as a means of trying to change Perry's behavior. Why didn't it work? There are many potential explanations.

First of all, it doesn't appear that Perry's teacher has ever used a time out before. Her students didn't even know what a time out was. Further, there wasn't even a predetermined time out area. Moreover, the teacher didn't give Perry a warning, so he didn't even understand what consequences his behavior would have.

The biggest reason that the time out strategy didn't work is that the punishment didn't match the crime. Think about it. Perry is getting in trouble for not remaining in his seat. So what does the teacher do? She makes him sit in the corner! What is more, if he can't remain in his time out chair, he will be sent to the principal, which apparently happened.

Question 2: How Could Self-Monitoring or Self-Questioning Have Worked in Perry's Situation?

Rather than using a time out strategy, Perry's teacher might have tried something more related to the cause of Perry's behavior, such as self-monitoring or self-questioning. One of the problems that children with ADHD have is that they do not pay attention to what they are doing. It is quite likely that Perry wants to behave but simply doesn't realize that he is getting out of his chair as often as he does. By using self-monitoring or self-questioning strategies, Perry can become more in tune with his actions. This will certainly help him in many ways other than staying seated.

To implement these strategies, the teacher could have Perry keep track of the number of times he gets out of his seat without permission. Further, throughout the day, Perry could also ask himself questions such as, "Am I doing what I should be doing?" or "Am I disturbing anybody?" The teacher could even set up a reward system that would encourage Perry to decrease the number of times that he gets out of his seat.

Question 3: Other Than Trying to Change Perry's Behavior, What Else Could the Teacher Have Done?

Remember, not every behavior needs to be changed, especially those behaviors that a child can't control. This might be the case with Perry. So, other than using behavioral modification, what else could Perry's teacher have done?

As with many behaviors caused by a disability, sometimes it is better simply to ignore the behavior. Perry doesn't seem to be harming or distracting anybody. The teacher is probably getting upset because she thinks Perry is going out of his way to annoy her. But this is probably not the case. Once she realizes this, she will be able to address her reaction to Perry's behavior rather than the behavior itself.

She might also have tried to accommodate Perry's behavior. For example, she could have used more active teaching strategies. Maybe she could even let him stand up in the back of the room when he couldn't sit down any longer. Perry could still learn even though he is standing! Moreover, he could use a drafting table to do his work and stand at the same time.

9

STRATEGIES FOR ADDRESSING SPECIFIC BEHAVIORS

CHAPTER OBJECTIVES

By the time you complete this chapter, you should be able to:

- Identify potential causes for several common behavior problems.
- Identify strategies that could address common behavior problems.

CASE STUDY OF STELLA GLADDEN

"I am a little concerned about your daughter Stella," Mr. Hernandez told Stella's mother and father during their parent-teacher meeting. "She is very quiet."

"Oh," Mrs. Gladden said with some relief. "I was afraid that you were going to say that she was misbehaving or failing your class."

"She has always been a quiet girl," Mr. Gladden added.

"Well, it kind of worries me," Mr. Hernandez continued. "She is doing fine in my class. And she never misbehaves at all." He paused for a moment, trying to find a tactful way of expressing his thoughts. "You see . . . she doesn't appear to have any friends. I mean, people don't hate her or anything, but I have never seen her interact with her peers even when I assign a small group activity. Does she have any friends outside of school?"

The Gladdens thought for a moment.

"There is Lisa," Mr. Gladden said. "I think that is her name."

"It was Leslie," corrected Mrs. Gladden, "but I don't think that they have seen much of each other since last summer. Why are you concerned?"

"Well," Mr. Hernandez said, shifting uncomfortably in his seat. "I am sure there is nothing to worry about, but . . . Did you hear about what happened to Jamie Owens?"

"Oh yes! Tragic," Mrs. Gladden gasped. Then she seemed to understand what Mr. Hernandez was hinting at. "But Stella would never do that. She isn't depressed or anything. She is just very quiet by nature."

"I know. However, I really think that she could benefit from having more friends and being more socially involved."

"We've tried to encourage her to join a team sport or a club," Mr. Gladden nodded, appearing to understand the seriousness of the discussion. "But she just doesn't seem interested in making friends."

CASE STUDY QUESTIONS

Question 1: What could be causing Stella's behavior?
Question 2: How can a behavioral modification program help Stella?
Question 3: What strategies might help Stella?

INTRODUCTION

In chapter 8 we discussed generic strategies that you could build into your behavioral modification programs. However, you might be wondering how to handle specific behaviors. In this chapter we discuss strategies for very common behavioral problems, including:

- Hyperactivity
- Inattentiveness

- Stereotypic behavior
- Withdrawn behavior
- Temper tantrums

(Please note that, due to their seriousness, aggressive and violent behaviors are covered separately in chapter 10.)

Many of these behaviors are associated with specific disabilities, such as various behavioral, cognitive, and attention disorders. However, this does not mean that everybody who demonstrates these behaviors has a disability. After all, not every child who has problems paying attention should be in special education. Wherever possible, multiple strategies are suggested based on potential causes for each behavior.

HYPERACTIVITY

With the recent increase in the diagnosis of attention deficit hyperactivity disorder (ADHD), hyperactivity has become a common problem faced by teachers and parents alike. However, hyperactivity is not simply getting out of one's seat or fidgeting. There are many behaviors associated with hyperactivity that parents and teachers may wish to target, including (but not limited to):

- Poor organizational skills
- Messy rooms or desks
- Rushing through work and making careless mistakes
- Poor social skills
- Talking too fast

It should be noted that not all children who are hyperactive have ADHD. In fact, only approximately 5 percent of the general population has attention disorders. Other causes of hyperactivity include:

- fetal alcohol effects (FAE)
- bipolar disorders
- drug use (e.g., stimulants)
- social immaturity

- being defiant
- being bored

There are many strategies that can help children who are hyperactive; however, you must first determine what is causing the problems. For example, if a child is bored in class, whether because she is gifted or is academically frustrated, you might want to consider changing the difficulty of the material presented. Perhaps allow gifted students to proceed ahead of the class at their own pace. Or give struggling students more concrete examples or one-on-one help. On the other hand, if a child is hyperactive because of drug use, counseling might be an appropriate treatment.

Children with biological causes for their hyperactivity may benefit from medication. However, studies have found that medication in and of itself is not as effective as a multiple-pronged approach. For instance, medication should be combined with behavioral modification and accommodations.

Rather than trying to force a hyperactive child to sit still, sometimes it is best to allow children to expel energy in an appropriate way. After all, a child with a lot of energy can be taught to be extremely productive rather than disruptive. The trick is to find ways of getting rid of pent up energy that will not disrupt others, such as:

- Having the child wiggle his toes instead of bouncing his knees or fidgeting back and forth in his seat.
- Having the child perform constructive activities, such as handing out papers, cleaning the chalkboard, or helping with household chores.
- Having the child get up and stretch.
- Having the child get daily exercise.
- Using teaching strategies that are active and hands on.
- Reinforcing being able to sit still a minute longer each day

When a child is hyperactive because of biological factors, you probably shouldn't use punishment. After all, she cannot control her body's need to move. It would be like punishing a student with mental retardation because she can't learn as quickly as her peers. In the end, both you and the child will become more and more frustrated.

INATTENTIVENESS

Inattentive students will frequently perform poorly in class because they miss important details, make careless mistakes, forget to complete assignments, or lose things. They may also have problems socially. For example, they may forget people's names, not attend to significant nonverbal communication, and have difficulty maintaining conversations.

Inattentiveness is another key characteristic of ADHD. However, as with hyperactivity, not every child who has difficulty paying attention has ADHD. There are an incalculable number of causes of such behavior, including:

- Depression
- Schizophrenia
- Hearing impairments
- Seizures
- Hypoglycemia
- Drug use
- Noncompliance
- Being bored
- Being tired

As with any behavior, you will want to figure out the cause of inattentiveness prior to intervening. For instance, students who are depressed, schizophrenic, and epileptic can often be treated effectively through the use of medications. However, there are some potentially effective strategies for addressing the behavior of inattentive children who do not require medication, such as:

- Teaching using hands-on activities
- Varying the type of instruction frequently
- Keeping presentation of information as brief as possible
- Using multiple modalities at the same time (e.g., using overheads to supplement lectures)
- Teaching the child active learning strategies (e.g., paraphrasing what has been said)
- Removing potential distractions

When presented with a child who does not pay attention, people frequently want to use some sort of reward or punishment program. For instance, they may give the child something that she likes if she increases the length of time she attends (i.e., positive reinforcement). Or perhaps they take away things that the child likes every time she doesn't pay attention (i.e., response-cost). Unfortunately, these strategies frequently do not work because it is very difficult to determine when a child is paying attention.

Think about it. How would you know whether your child was paying attention to you? Because she is staring at you when you are talking? Because she is nodding her head? Because she can repeat the last thing that you said? None of these behaviors indicates that your child is actually paying attention. She could be staring right through you daydreaming, for all you know.

Therefore, when working with children with attention problems, it is best to focus on observable outcomes of attention. For example, you could try to increase their grades or the completion of their work by an assigned deadline. These are much better target behaviors than making a child stare at you when you are talking. Moreover, by focusing on grades or completion of tasks, you are focusing on behaviors that really matter. After all, inattention in and of itself is not a problem; it is the consequences of inattention, such as walking into traffic or constantly losing car keys, that pose the greatest concern.

STEREOTYPIC BEHAVIOR

If you have watched movies such as *Rainman* or *As Good As It Gets*, you probably have seen examples of stereotypic behavior. Stereotypic behavior usually involves repetitious behaviors that occur at a very high rate. Examples of stereotypic behavior include:

- rocking back and forth,
- flapping their hands in front of their eyes,
- stroking their arms,
- twirling their fingers, and
- bouncing up and down.

It is difficult to say with any degree of certainty what causes stereotypic behaviors. They do not have any apparent function. However, they may be a learned behavior used to calm the child down when anxious. They may also be caused by biological factors, such as abnormal development of the brain or central nervous system.

Stereotypic behaviors are commonly associated with:

- Autism
- Asperger's disorder
- Obsessive-compulsive disorders
- Anxiety disorders
- ADHD
- Sensory impairments

When a stereotypic behavior involves self-injury, you should first take precautions to ensure the safety of the child. Children with self-injurious behaviors (SIBs) frequently wear helmets or padding that prevent them from causing themselves harm. You can then work on reducing the causes of the behavior (e.g., excessive noise) and then on systematically improving tolerance by slowly increasing exposure to the trigger.

Often mildly annoying stereotypic behavior can be overlooked or accommodated. Unless the behavior severely affects your child's social abilities or the behavior is physically harmful, you may not need to intervene. If the behaviors are simply bothering to you, you may wish to employ stress reduction techniques, such as taking breaks away from the child and deep breathing.

WITHDRAWN BEHAVIOR

Too often parents and teachers are only concerned about aggressive or annoying behavior such as getting into fights or making inappropriate comments. But children who are socially withdrawn could benefit from behavioral modification as well. However, as with all behaviors, you will first have to identify the cause of the behavior before you can change it.

Withdrawn behavior can be associated with many conditions, including:

- Physical, emotional, or sexual abuse
- Anxiety disorders
- Depression
- Selective mutism
- Drug and alcohol use
- Being naturally shy

Children who are withdrawn may exhibit a wide range of target behaviors. They may not speak much or may refuse to play with their
peers. They may appear socially awkward and have few friends. They
might also have underdeveloped communication skills.

Strategies for helping children who are withdrawn vary depending on
the cause. Children who are withdrawn because of anxiety or depression
may respond well to medications. These children, as well as children
who are naturally shy, have been abused, or have selective mutism, may
also benefit from counseling.

Additional strategies for helping children who are socially withdrawn
include:

- Social skills training
- Rewarding a gradual increase of peer interaction
- Using activities that require interactions
- Building self-esteem
- Role playing appropriate social interactions

TEMPER TANTRUMS

Most parents or teachers of young children have experienced the
dreaded temper tantrum. Temper tantrums are extremely frustrating
not only for the child's teachers and parents but for those nearby as well.
Imagine being trapped on a long plane or bus ride with a screaming
child! However, giving into a screaming child, while ending the immediate tantrum, will only promote the behavior in the long run. As a result, effective behavioral modification strategies are necessary not only

to decrease the frequency and intensity of tantrums but also to teach children appropriate social skills.

Temper tantrums are typically characterized by screaming, noncompliance, and aggressive behavior. During tantrums, children usually are illogical and out of control. Further, these behaviors continue over a prolonged period of time.

Developmentally, it might be appropriate for very young children to get upset, fall to the floor, and kick or scream once in a while. However, if these behaviors are extremely frequent or severe in nature, they may be atypical and need to be addressed. Further, by age four or five most children should be able to self-regulate their own behaviors to conform to parental expectations.

The purpose of temper tantrums is usually to get something, such as attention or a prized object. They often occur shortly after being told "no" or having something taken away. Knowing when tantrums tend to erupt will help parents and teachers prevent them. This is not to say that parents and teachers should avoid situations in which they say "no" to children. But knowing what triggers the behavior enables parents and teachers to redirect the child before he or she becomes irrational and defiant.

For example, suppose that your daughter is likely to get upset when you tell her to stop playing and get ready for dinner. If you just say, "Stop playing, it is dinner time," she will likely react negatively to your instruction. However, if you warn her that dinner will be ready in 15 minutes and then redirect her inside the house, perhaps under the pretense of wanting to show her something or get her opinion on what you have just cooked, she might be less likely to throw a temper tantrum.

In addition to redirection, there are a number of other methods of addressing temper tantrums that can be very effective, including:

- Being consistent in how temper tantrums are handled
- Rewarding appropriate behavior (e.g., asking for something nicely)
- Using time out strategies
- Extinction (e.g., allowing the behavior to continue until the child is exhausted)
- After the tantrum, discussing what happened and how the child should have acted

APPLYING WHAT YOU HAVE READ

In this chapter we discussed several common behavior problems that parents and teachers frequently face. We also discussed potential causes of these behaviors as well as potential strategies for addressing them. Now let's apply what you have learned. Go back and read the case study at the beginning of the chapter. Then attempt to answer the following questions.

Question 1: What Could Be Causing Stella's Behavior?

In almost every chapter of this book we have discussed the importance of knowing what causes behavior. Without understanding its cause, it would be very difficult to change your child's behavior. So what do you think is causing Stella's behavior?

There are many possible reasons why Stella isn't interacting with her peers. Perhaps she is depressed. Maybe her peers don't feel comfortable around her. Or maybe she is just very shy. What you think is causing Stella's behavior will guide how you help her.

Question 2: How Can a Behavioral Modification Program Help Stella?

Behavioral modification programs are not just for children with bad behaviors. Behavioral modification can help with many aspects of life, including study and social skills. How could you help Stella? If you were helping her, what would your behavioral modification program look like?

Before you can help Stella, you have to identify a target behavior that is measurable. Increasing the number of friends that she has would certainly help Stella, but how do you measure friends? You could have her identify who she considers are her friends, but that doesn't mean they actually are. Focusing on the amount of time that she speaks in class or to her classmates might be more appropriate.

Next you will need to figure out why she is having difficulty speaking to her classmates. Is it because she lacks social skills? Is she depressed? As discussed previously, your hypothesis will determine your actions.

Finally, based on your guess about the cause of her behavior, you would want to intervene in some way. Perhaps reward Stella for every time she talked. Maybe take away points for not participating. You would then compare the frequency of the target behavior (i.e., talking to peers) before the intervention (i.e., baseline) to its frequency after you start intervening. If there is a significant increase, you could conclude that it was due to your behavioral modification program. If there isn't an increase, or the increase isn't as big as you would like, then you might want to reconsider your intervention.

Question 3: What Strategies Might Help Stella?

There are a number of strategies that could be used to help children like Stella interact more with their peers. For instance, the teacher could use group activities or projects that require students to collaborate. Stella could play a team sport or join a club that she likes. She could get a pen pal. She might not be able to interact face to face with a pen pal, but she could still make friends. The possibilities are limitless.

10

PREVENTING, DE-ESCALATING, AND REACTING TO AGGRESSIVE BEHAVIORS

CHAPTER OBJECTIVES

By the time you complete this chapter, you should be able to:

- Outline the various stages of aggressive behavior.
- Indicate the proper responses to children in each stage.
- Prevent and de-escalate aggressive behavior.
- List what not to wear around aggressive children.
- Describe what to do if a child attacks you.

CASE STUDY OF LAURANA JERGEN

Despite being one of the smallest girls in her class, Laurana is the terror of her preschool. Teachers live in fear of being around Laurana when she is upset, which is far too frequently for those around her. She will bite, kick, hit, grab, and throw things. She has even stabbed a teacher's aide with a sharpened pencil.

In an effort to decrease her violent behavior, Laurana's parents and teachers developed a behavioral modification plan whereby she was rewarded for being nice to people and punished for being aggressive.

Unfortunately, as the plan was being implemented, Laurana's behaviors increased, both in terms of frequency and their severity. Nearly every day she injured somebody in her class.

One day Laurana was upset because another child had taken her favorite toy. Seeing that Laurana was going to be thrown into one of her uncontrollable fits, her teacher stepped in and tried to defuse the situation.

"Laurana, if you don't calm down I will take away all of your toys!" Her teacher told her in a very stern voice.

"But she took my rabbit," Laurana screamed, pointing to the little girl who was holding a white stuffed rabbit. "She took my rabbit! She took my rabbit!" Laurana repeated over and over in a high-pitched shrill.

The little girl looked terrified and was offering to give it back to Laurana, but the teacher stopped her.

"No, Brandy," she said to the little girl. "Keep the rabbit. It isn't Laurana's. It belongs to the class. She needs to learn how to share."

Almost immediately Laurana began to scream and kick things across the room.

The teacher walked up to Laurana, knelt down, and pointed her finger at Laurana so that it was inches away from her nose.

"Now you settle down, or I mean it. You won't be allowed to play with any toys for the rest of the day."

As quick as lightning, Laurana bit the teacher's finger and kicked her in the knee. The teacher pulled away, leaving some of her finger behind in Laurana's mouth. Laurana then grabbed the teacher's necklace and began to twist. Seeing that the she needed help, two classroom aides ran to the teacher's side and pulled Laurana off her.

CASE STUDY QUESTIONS

Question 1: What stage of behavior was Laurana in when the teacher intervened?

Question 2: How could the teacher have prepared for Laurana's aggressive behaviors even before they began?

Question 3: What should the teacher have done during Laurana's violent behavior?

INTRODUCTION

Gone are the days when the worst thing that parents and teachers had to worry about was a child talking back to them or chewing gum in class. Nowadays, violence has entered even the once safe confines of the elementary school. It is sad but true. Just watch the news. It seems that few days go by without a student bringing a gun to school or being expelled for assaulting other students or teachers. Even little children have been known to become very violent. For this reason, parents and teachers need to be able to deal with potential aggressive behaviors.

Don't think of "violence" as "deadly," although this can certainly be the case, as the nation saw at Columbine and other schools. Think of violence as any unwanted physical contact, such as pushing, grabbing, hair pulling, biting, or hitting. Such behaviors can be dealt with in the manner outlined in the previous chapters. However, sometimes aggressive behavior has to be dealt with right when the behavior is happening.

This chapter addresses many of the issues that arise as a result of having a child who is potentially violent. Particular emphasis is given to preventing aggressive behavior as well as minimizing physical injuries that could result. However, please realize that while the information presented in this chapter will be helpful, you should consider taking a class on self-defense. Many school districts and community programs offer such classes to teachers and parents.

PROTECTING YOURSELF BEFORE AGGRESSION OCCURS

Too many victims of violence do not think about protecting themselves before the violent act occurs. This is very unfortunate, especially since many injuries can be prevented with a little bit of forethought and planning. Below we discuss some very simple strategies that you might want to use before you ever start working with children.

What to Wear

Take a moment to look at what you are wearing. Look at your shoes, how you are wearing your hair, your jewelry. Now ask yourself, "How can what I am wearing affect how I react to an aggressive student?" You probably have never thought about how what you wear could affect a potentially dangerous situation, but it can.

There are definitely some do's and don'ts when it comes to what you wear around children who are potentially aggressive. For example, you want to wear clothing that enables you to move around freely. Imagine trying to run away in high heels or cowboy boots! You probably wouldn't get very far very fast.

You also do not want to wear watches with metal bands or rings with high stone settings. These can cut both you and the child if things become physical. If you have a ring with a high stone setting, such as an engagement ring, and you don't want to take it off all of the time, you can buy clear rubber band-like devices that go around the edge of the stone. Because they are small and clear, you can barely see them, but they do a good job of preventing the ring from getting snagged on clothes or cutting a child whom you are trying to restrain. Long fingernails can also cause damage.

You probably should also not wear earrings, especially large hoop earrings. A child could grab them and rip them right through your ears— taking off a large chunk of your earlobe. This can happen with little children. There have been cases of infants reaching up, grabbing somebody's shiny earrings, and accidentally pulling the earring down through the lobe.

Necklaces can also be problematic. First of all, you shouldn't wear anything that you wouldn't mind getting broken. Second, you shouldn't wear anything that won't break. Imagine if you had a thick necklace on and somebody grabbed it. All he or she would have to do is twist it around his or her fist and you wouldn't be able to breathe. You would probably start to panic within seconds.

Men's ties are even worse than necklaces. They don't break, and they can easily be turned into a noose. This is why many police officers wear clip-on ties. If somebody grabs them, they will come off.

How about your hair? Can your hair be a potential liability? Yes, especially if it is long and free-flowing. One of the easiest parts of the body to hurt, and the toughest to repair, is the neck. All somebody has to do is grab your hair and tug on it and you could have a life-altering injury, just as if you got whiplash from a minor car accident.

Having curly hair, in particular, can be dangerous. If you have curly hair, slide your fingers into it and look in the mirror. What do you see? Chances are, your hair has automatically wrapped itself around your fingers, making it very easy to grab. In fact, somebody might grab your hair and find it difficult to let go because his or her fingers have become so entangled in your curls.

Now you shouldn't go shave your head, throw out all your jewelry, or go around barefoot. However, you might want to think a little bit about what you are wearing and how it might affect how you can respond in an emergency. Consider wearing your hair up or in a ponytail, which is harder to grab. You can also wear a hat. Maybe wear slacks instead of skirts, or wear comfortable shoes in which you can run if need be. Get a watch with a leather or plastic band. Again, it is up to you, but any chance to minimize potential injury might be worth considering. In summary, here are a few things to avoid if you are working with children:

- Watches with metal bands
- Rings with high stone settings
- Earrings—especially hoop earrings
- Necklaces that you do not want broken
- Shoes you cannot run in (high heels, sandals, boots)
- Skirts in which you could not run
- Skirts that prevent you from being on the floor
- Long, free-flowing hair
- Ties (unless clip-ons)
- Long fingernails

Environmental Factors

In addition to fashion, you should also consider your environment when working with potentially aggressive children. Look around where you are right now. What do you notice? Where are the exits? Are there any objects that could be used as a weapon, such as sharpened pencils or chairs that are light enough to be thrown? Some of these objects should probably be removed when children with a history of violence are in the room.

Also consider objects in the room that can help you. For example, if there is a big heavy table, you could keep the table in between you and the violent person. Is there a phone that you can use to call for help? Are there people within shouting distance?

Mental Planning

Look around the room again and think about what you would do if somebody came in the room and tried to attack you right this moment. Where would you go? How would you defend yourself? Are there any objects in the room that could hurt you if thrown or used as a weapon?

These are things that you should consider whenever you are with a child who gets aggressive. In fact, you can make mental planning a kind of a game. Whenever you are bored and standing in line some place, make it a practice to look around and think to yourself, "Hmmm, what would I do if somebody jumped out from those bushes? Or out from the shadows?" The best defense against aggressive behavior is to be ready for it.

PREVENTING AGGRESSIVE BEHAVIOR

Preventing aggressive behavior is just as important as reacting correctly to it. Like most behavior, aggression is usually caused by something. People typically do not suddenly fly off the handle and start hitting or kicking. There probably is some sort of cause of the behavior. In this case, you can use the steps that we outlined throughout the earlier chapters to help determine what is causing the behavior.

Keep in mind that aggressive behavior is an effective method of communication. So your child might be trying to tell you something, especially if he is nonverbal or has mental retardation. Think about it. If you were not able to talk and you were in pain or sitting in urine-soaked pants, but nobody noticed, how would you get someone's attention? You would probably grab someone. If that didn't work, you would probably use more assertive methods. So, when working with children who tend to be aggressive and have communication difficulties, try to understand that they might be trying to tell you something. Use the process outlined in chapter 4 to figure out what the child is trying to tell you when she becomes violent.

DE-ESCALATING AGGRESSIVE BEHAVIOR

As discussed briefly before, people usually don't suddenly go from being pleasant to being violent. There is a series of stages that people go through before they become violent. They may skip a step or go back and forth between steps, but people's behavior can often be predicted. Further, if you can recognize the earlier stages and respond accordingly, you can often de-escalate the situation before it becomes physical. The stages (see table 10.1) are:

Stage 1: Normal
Stage 2: Tension
Stage 3: Defensive
Stage 4: Aggressive
Stage 5: Release
Stage 6: Reintegration

Normal

The normal stage is the way that the child usually behaves. This, of course, varies from person to person. Maybe he tends to be shy, or happy, or energetic, or whatever. At this stage, you would treat the child as you always would—hopefully with love and respect.

Tension

At the beginning of the tension stage, something has changed the child's behavior. Perhaps somebody said something mean or sarcastic.

Table 10.1 Stages of Violent Behavior and the Appropriate Responses

Stages	Response
Stage #1: Normal	Treat child with love and respect
Stage #2: Tension	Divert attention. Remove triggers. Allow to vent.
Stage #3: Defensive	Allow to vent. Set clear, concise, and enforceable limits.
Stage #4: Aggressive	Prevent child from hurting herself or others
Stage #5: Release	Help child to regain composure
Stage #6: Reintegration	Talk to the child about their behavior and how they should have behaved

Or the child saw something that bothered her. Something triggered the change in behavior. If you can identify this trigger, you can avoid it or teach the child how to deal with it, thus preventing aggressive behavior in the future.

When your child enters the tension stage, you will probably notice a subtle change in the way that she is acting. Rather than her normal state, she might become quieter. Her fists or jaw might clench. She might also fidget back and forth or look uncomfortable.

Once you recognize that your child is in the tension stage, there are several things that you can do to return her to the normal stage. First, remove the trigger. For example, if she is being bothered by another child, separate them.

Second, have the child talk about what she is feeling. Talking is a great way of releasing tension. Also, it could improve her communication skills.

When the child is talking, genuinely listen to what she has to say. Don't fake it or be condescending. Also, be supportive, not judgmental. This is the time to let your child vent. Don't point out how she is wrong or how other people might feel differently in the same situation. Just let her talk.

Another effective strategy for de-escalating a child who is in this stage is to redirect his attention. Perhaps distract him by talking about something that you know he likes. Maybe ask him to do something that would be pleasant for him. Try anything that would get his mind off the trigger. However, the distraction must be positive from the child's perspective. If you try to redirect him with something that he finds undesirable, such as doing his homework, you will probably escalate his behavior.

Defensive

After the tension stage comes the defensive stage. Here, your child will begin to lose rational thinking and become noncompliant. She might begin to yell and take everything very personally. She will seem focused on the same topic and you will have difficulty diverting her attention.

There are several ways to handle a child who is being defensive. The first is to continue to let her vent. Talking is much better than physical aggression. Again, try to get her away from the trigger and allow her to explain why she is upset.

However, children at the defensive stage frequently will not be able to have a rational conversation or control their behavior. If your child's behavior continues to escalate, be directive. Set limits that are clear, concise, and enforceable. Don't say something like, "You better calm down or you will be grounded for life!" Both you and your child know that is an exaggeration.

Instead, say something that is more reasonable, such as "You can either calm down and stay here, or go up to your bedroom." It is important to emphasize the positive behavior that you want the child to perform, not the negative behavior that you want him to stop doing. In addition, giving choices is a way that your child can "save face" as well as feel that he is in charge.

Aggressive

Once children pass the defensive stage, they may become physically aggressive. At this stage, they have lost physical control and rationality. Reasoning with them will probably not be effective, nor will being directive. If they are a danger to themselves, others, or their environment (e.g., destroying property), you will need to either restrain them or call for help.

It would be difficult to learn how to restrain violent students from reading a book. If you have violent children, it would be advantageous for you to become trained in how to safely restrain them. There are several national organizations that provide wonderful training on this topic (see www.crisisprevention.com).

Release

When you were a child, did you ever throw a temper tantrum? How long did it last? Do you remember being physically and emotionally exhausted afterward?

Being aggressive takes an enormous amount of energy. Children cannot continue acting out indefinitely. At some point, they will reach their limit. This is the stage called release. It is characterized by the child behaving close to normally. She may cry or apologize or simply collapse.

At this stage it is important to help the child regain her composure. Be supportive and reassuring. Now is not the time to talk about punishments or her behavior. Give her time to regain control and to process what has just happened. Time out rooms can be very effective if they are used as a way for children to relax and not as a punishment.

Reintegration

Reintegration occurs after the child has returned to normal. This is the "teaching moment" when both of you can sit down and talk about what caused the behavior and how the child should have acted. Through these discussions, both you and your child should learn something about the behavior and how to prevent it in the future.

WHAT TO DO IF YOU ARE ATTACKED

Although it would be impossible to teach you how to safely restrain your child simply by reading this chapter, you can learn a few pointers to protect yourself should you be attacked. In this section, we will discuss what to do if a child tries to:

- bite,
- kick or hit
- pull your hair,
- grab, or
- choke.

Please note that before performing the strategies outlined in this section, you should be trained by a professional. Further, the strategies that are suggested are considered "nonharmful" for the attacker. There may be times when you are attacked by a child when you need to use whatever force is necessary to get out of the situation.

Bites

Bites from humans are actually very dangerous. Not only do our mouths have many germs that can infect wounds that break the skin, but there is a high likelihood of significant damage. It is very important that you protect yourself from being bitten.

The best way to avoid being bitten, of course, is not to allow an angry child close enough to touch you. This is what is called maintaining "personal space," which tends to be an arm's length away from the other person. This, however, is not always practical.

The worst thing that you can do if you are bitten is to pull away. Why? Ever take a bite of a chicken or turkey leg? What happens if you pull the leg away from your mouth when you haven't bitten completely through the meat? The entire piece of meat is pulled from the bone. The same could happen if somebody bit you and you pulled away from that person suddenly. The muscle and tendons can actually be severed from the bone, causing tremendous damage, not to mention pain.

The first thing that you should do if somebody bites you is to immobilize the person's head. Do whatever you can to prevent him from pulling away with a hunk of you still in his mouth. You could grab his head with your hand and hold it to you. Or, if the person bites you in the back or some place that you cannot reach, back him up against a wall. Again, the main thing is to prevent the person from pulling away while still biting you.

Further, instead of pulling away, try pushing the body part that the person is biting deeper into his mouth. This will make that person gag. When someone gags, his mouth will open automatically. You can also apply pressure at the corner of the biter's mouth where his teeth meet the hinge of the jaw. This can pop the jaw open. Grabbing the nose and pulling upward can also work.

Once you are able, clean all bites right away. If the bite breaks the skin, consult your doctor. You may need to have a tetanus shot if you haven't had one recently.

Kicks and Hits

Being kicked or hit can be just as serious as being bitten. Imagine getting kicked in the knee. Knees are very easily damaged. They are also very difficult to repair. One kick to the knee could affect your mobility for the rest of your life. Getting hit in the eye could affect your vision for the rest of your life, also. So how do you prevent being kicked or hit? As we said earlier, keeping your distance is your first line of defense. Remember, to kick you, your child would have to shift his weight, bring his foot back, and then kick you. If you pay attention to his body language, you should have enough time to evade the blow.

So you are paying attention to your child's body language. You are keeping your distance. You see your child shifting his weight and drawing his foot back. What should you do? You can do one of two things, block or move.

To block a kick, shift your weight on to your back foot. Then bring your front foot up to approximately knee-level of your child. Use the bottom of your foot to deflect your child's kick. At the very least, this should protect your knee and groin area.

Instead of blocking, you might want to move out of the way. But in what direction should you move? Think about this for a moment. Imagine that somebody is standing in front of you and is about to kick you. If you move backward, you may still be within range of his or her leg. So it is actually easier, and much quicker, to move to the side.

Hair Pulling

Although it may sound like a trivial way of assaulting somebody, hair pulling can be very dangerous. If somebody pulls your hair, your head is likely to jerk in an unnatural manner. Consequently, you can hurt your neck, much as if you were in a car accident. As with whiplash, injuries to the neck are extremely difficult to fix and could cause you a lifetime of pain.

As with any assault, the first defense against hair pulling is not to let people close enough to grab your hair. Further, as discussed previously, you may not want to have your hair free-flowing. Pony tails and buns can reduce the likelihood of somebody being able to grab your hair.

If a violent child does manage to grab your hair, the first thing to do is to immobilize her hand. Prevent her from pulling away by grabbing her wrist or maneuvering her into a corner. Next, apply pressure between her knuckles. This should pop open her grip. However, there may be times when a person wants to let go of your hair but can't because it is wrapped around her fingers. This is particularly common if you have curly hair. If you cannot get free, continue to immobilize the hand and call for help.

Grabs

If you have children, you undoubtedly have been grabbed at some point and probably on many locations of your body. However, in this section we are not talking about grabs that are meant to get your attention. Instead, we focus on what to do when somebody grabs you violently, perhaps with intent to harm you.

Take one of your hands and grab your other wrist. Look at the grip. Do you see where your fingers and thumb almost meet? That is the weak point of the grip. Rather than trying to pull straight back, you should try to break through where the fingers meet. You can do this by twisting and pulling.

You are probably saying to yourself, "Sure, that is good and fine, but what if somebody grabs me with both hands?" The principles are basically the same. Have somebody grab your arm with both hands. Look at the person's grip. It is impossible to grab somebody with two hands and not have a weak spot. Can you see it? It should be where fingers or thumbs overlap.

Once you have identified the weak part of the grip, twist and pull through as you did with a one-handed grip. You may have to use your other hand to help you pull through. You can also use momentum. Twist with your entire body.

Now you are probably thinking, "What if someone grabs me some place other than the arm? What do I do then?" If somebody grabs an article of clothing, such as a sleeve, or a body part that you can reach, apply pressure in between his knuckles. This should open up his grip.

Choking

Choking is just like grabbing. There is a weak part of the grip that makes it very easy to break free. However, you get out of chokeholds a little differently than you do from simple grabs. Imagine that somebody has her hands on your throat. Clearly, this is a potentially dangerous situation. To get free, you can do one of two things.

You could bring your arms straight up, as if you are signaling for a touchdown, and then twist your entire body away from the attacker. The momentum from your shoulder should break the person's grip. You should also be a step or two away from your attacker, thus enabling you to run.

Another way of breaking free when somebody is grabbing your throat is to swing your arms like a windmill. Swing your arms up over the person's arms and then bring them down hard, knocking the attacker's arms downward. This maneuver, however, is only useful if the person is in front of you.

APPLYING WHAT YOU HAVE READ

Because of the seriousness of the topic, this entire chapter is dedicated to addressing aggressive behavior. You should consider being trained in nonviolent crisis prevention techniques, but for now, let's apply what you have read. Go back and read the case study at the beginning of the chapter and then answer the following questions.

Question 1: What Stage of Behavior Was Laurana in When the Teacher Intervened?

As we discussed in this chapter, aggressive children aren't always aggressive. Further, they usually progress through a series of more or less predictable stages before they become violent. What stage was Laurana in when her teacher intervened?

From what is written in the case study, Laurana was normal before she saw that another girl was playing with her favorite toy. This was the trigger to Laurana's escalating behavior. When the teacher intervened, Laurana was passing the tension stage and becoming more defensive. She clearly was losing control and did not have a handle on her own behavior.

Question 2: How Could the Teacher Have Prepared for Laurana's Aggressive Behaviors Even Before They Began?

When working with children who have a history of aggressive behavior, teachers and parents need to be prepared even before the behaviors occur. This includes making sure that you wear the right things and don't wear the wrong things. How should the teacher have prepared for Laurana's aggressive behavior?

One thing that the teacher should have done was not wear a necklace. Necklaces can be used to choke people, as the teacher found out. Ties too can be very dangerous. If you are going to wear something around your neck, make sure that it would break away if somebody grabbed it.

Question 3: What Should the Teacher Have Done During Laurana's Violent Behavior?

Knowing how to de-escalate behavior before it turns violent is an immensely valuable skill. But knowing how to respond as a child turns violent is also very important. What should the teacher have done when Laurana started to attack her?

The teacher should not have pulled away when Laurana bit her finger. This can cause more damage. Further, the teacher would have been wise to keep her distance when confronting Laurana. Had she been a few feet away, Laurana couldn't have kicked or bitten her, let alone choked her with her necklace.

ABOUT THE AUTHOR

Robert Evert Cimera, Ph.D., is an associate professor of Special Education at the University of Wisconsin at Oshkosh. He specializes in the areas of lifelong transition and attention deficit hyperactivity disorders (ADHD). In addition to this book, he has also written *Making ADHD a Gift: Teaching Superman How to Fly; Preparing Children with Disabilities for Life;* and *The Truth about Special Education: A Guide for Parents and Teachers.*